Input-Based Incremental Vocabulary Instruction

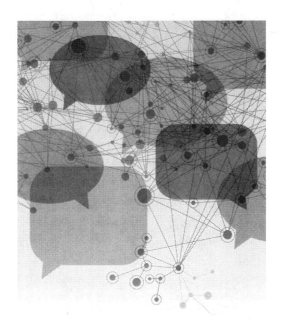

Joe Barcroft

tesol
international
association

Typeset in ITC New Baskerville and Optima
by Capitol Communications, LLC, Crofton, Maryland USA
and printed by Gasch Printing, LLC, Odenton, Maryland 21113

TESOL International Association
1925 Ballenger Avenue
Alexandria, Virginia 22314 USA
Tel 703-836-0774 • Fax 703-836-7864 • info@tesol.org • www.tesol.org

Publishing Manager: Carol Edwards
Copy Editor: Sarah J. Duffy
Cover Design: Citrine Sky Design, Edgewater, Maryland USA

TESOL Book Publications Committee
            John I. Liontas, Chair
Maureen S. Andrade   Joe McVeigh
Jennifer Lebedev   Gail Schafers
Robyn L. Brinks Lockwood   Lynn Zimmerman

Project overview: John I. Liontas and Maureen S. Andrade

ISBN 9781931185752
Library of Congress Control Number 2012948624

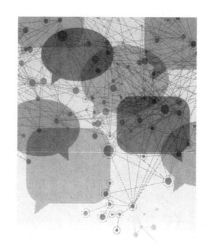

Input-Based Incremental
Vocabulary Instruction

Joe Barcroft

Ten Principles of Effective Vocabulary Instruction

1. Develop and implement a vocabulary acquisition plan.

2. Present new words frequently and repeatedly in the input.

3. Promote both intentional and incidental vocabulary learning.

4. Use meaning-bearing comprehensible input when presenting new words.

5. Present new words in an enhanced manner.

6. Limit forced output without access to meaning during the initial stages.

7. Limit forced semantic elaboration during the initial stages.

8. Promote learning L2-specific word meanings and usage over time.

9. Progress from less demanding to more demanding activities over time.

10. Apply research findings with direct implications for vocabulary instruction.

Checklist for IBI Vocabulary Instruction Lessons

☐   1.   I decided on target vocabulary and materials needed for the activities.

☐   2.   I designed the activities to be meaningful, educational, and interactive.

☐   3.   I included cultural and historical information when appropriate.

☐   4.   I made sure target vocabulary is presented repeatedly in the input first.

☐   5.   I increased the difficulty of tasks involving target vocabulary gradually over time.

☐   6.   I incorporated a number of the principles of the IBI approach.

☐   7. I included directly applicable research findings.

Dedication

This book is dedicated to James G. Durham—best friend anyone could ever have, thoughtful and informed world traveler, and law library deputy director par excellence (but in a parallel universe, gender studies researcher and goat farmer). James is the type of friend who understands what you want to talk about in about five seconds or less and always encourages you to move forward in the best way. Thanks, James.

Table of Contents

Acknowledgments

Besides the author, the person most responsible for the arrival of this book is Wynne Wong, who requested the first version of the manuscript of this book to be used as a primary text for a graduate seminar on second language vocabulary instruction at The Ohio State University. The manuscript has been used in two offerings of the seminar. I am very grateful to Wynne not only for her help in providing an initial impetus for writing the book but also for her consistent support and valuable feedback throughout the writing and revision process.

My appreciation also goes to Norbert Schmitt for his invaluable comments and encouragement at various stages of this project. Thank you also to TESOL Publications for accepting this project and especially to Carol Edwards, Publishing Manager at TESOL International Association, whose talent, cheerfulness, and encouragement made working on this project a delightful experience at every step of the way. My thanks also to the anonymous reviewers who helped shape the book manuscript and, in particular, to one anonymous reviewer working with TESOL Publications who provided a number of detailed suggestions for improving the book manuscript. Additionally, I am grateful to Leonardo Carvajal Gamarra for his practical commentary on the overall readability of the book manuscript.

Finally, I extend my gratitude to Jacqueline White Militello, Instructor in the English Language Program at Washington University in St. Louis, for her willingness to implement and provide helpful feedback on the approach to vocabulary instruction advocated in this book. Her dedication to her students and to effective language instruction, including careful attention to vocabulary development, is an inspiration.

CHAPTER 1

Getting Started With Five Key Questions

As both instructors and students know well, vocabulary is at the center of language acquisition and successful communication. Words and lexical phrases (recurring combinations of multiple words) are the fabric of language, the building blocks of what we use to communicate with one another. Limited vocabulary knowledge always restricts the ability to communicate in an effective manner. On the other hand, improving vocabulary knowledge can increase communicative competence by leaps and bounds. Not surprisingly, students of second languages (L2s) are particularly interested in receiving instruction on vocabulary (see James, 1996), identify vocabulary knowledge as the most important factor underlying successful communication with native speakers (Gorman, 1979), and point to lack of vocabulary knowledge as one of their principal sources of difficulty in the L2 (Meara, 1980). Advanced L2 learners also suffer from limited vocabulary knowledge, such as when it comes to their command of idiomatic expressions (see Arnaud & Savignon, 1997) and field-specific vocabulary (such as for business, medicine, law, botany). This type of limited vocabulary knowledge can be a burden year after year, persistently restricting the advanced L2 learner's ability to communicate in a more precise and effective manner.

VOCABULARY AND OTHER AREAS OF LINGUISTIC DEVELOPMENT

When it comes to the importance of vocabulary compared to other areas of linguistic development, as Wilkins (1972) pointed out, lack of grammatical knowledge may impede the ability to convey meaning, but absence of vocabulary can impede the ability to transmit meaning altogether. Consider, for example, the two types of errors in the sentences presented in Table 1.1. Notice how none of the sentences with grammatical errors impede comprehension of the speaker's intended meaning to the extent that the sentences with lexical errors do. Given this state of affairs, it is not surprising that native speakers identify vocabulary errors to be the most serious error and the greatest impediment to successful comprehension and vocabulary knowledge to be the *most important* aspect of language use (Politzer, 1978).

When assessing the importance of vocabulary, we must also consider the relationship between knowledge of individual words and knowledge of grammar.

Table 1.1 Comparisons of Grammatical and Lexical Errors in L2 Production

Language	Intended meaning	Grammatical error	Lexical error
English	She waited for me.	She waited me.	She hoped for me.
	I want to cash a check.	I want cash a check.	I want to change a check.
Spanish	*Estoy avergonzada.* "I am embarrassed."	*Yo avergonzada.* "I embarrassed."	*Estoy embarazada.* "I am pregnant."
	El lápiz está en el suelo. "The pencil is on the floor."	*El lápiz en el suelo.* "The pencil on the floor."	*El lápiz está en la flor.* "The pencil is on the flower."

Research suggests that much of what is called *grammatical knowledge* actually resides at the level of individual words. Healy and Sherrod (1994; see also Healy et al., 1998), for example, demonstrate that English speakers pronounce the word *the* using the schwa phoneme before consonant sounds (*the book, the front*) and the phoneme /i/ before vowel sounds (*the author, the inside*) based on information stored at the level of individual words that builds up gradually over time due to exposure to many exemplars of words. Serwatka and Healy (1998) found that the ability to distinguish between count and mass nouns in English is also based on word-level knowledge.

Additionally, Barcroft (2007b) found that the ability of native English speakers to make accurate grammaticality judgments decreased dramatically when they were asked to work with unreal words instead of real words. In this study, native English speakers were presented with sentences with dative alternation violations that contained polysyllabic verbs (**John explained Mary the plan*) using real verbs (*explained*), similar-to-real verbs (*explunned*), and dissimilar-to-real verbs (*tidnopped*) and sentences with comparative violations with polysyllabic adjectives (**Robert is demandinger than Allen*) using real adjectives (*demanding*), similar-to-real adjectives (*demunding*), and dissimilar-to-real adjectives (*natormunt*). Although the participants were asked to treat all unreal words as real words, their ability to reject the ungrammatical sentences decreased dramatically when the sentences contained unreal words (verbs or adjectives). The similar-to-real words led to performance that fell between the other two conditions, argued to be due to partial activation of their corresponding real words, at least in the case of the adjectives. The findings of this study (see Table 1.2; rejection rates are for all experimental sentences, not only the examples provided) further demonstrate that much of what is sometimes considered to be grammatical knowledge actually resides at the level of individual words.

All of these points regarding the central role of vocabulary in language acquisition and use suggest that vocabulary should also have a central role in the design and development of L2 programs and L2 teaching. However, L2 instruction and

Table 1.2 Examples of Real and Unreal Words Used in Sentences

Structure	Condition	Example of ungrammatical sentence	Rejection rate (%)
Multisyllabic verb	Real	John explained Mary the plan.	93
	Similar	John explunned Mary the plan.	32
	Dissimilar	John tidnopped Mary the plan.	29
Trisyllabic adjective	Real	Robert is demandinger than Allen.	87
	Similar	Robert is demundinger than Allen.	55
	Dissimilar	Robert is natormunter than Allen.	32

Source: Barcroft (2007b).

research on second language acquisition (SLA) traditionally have focused more on the acquisition of grammar than on vocabulary. According to Zimmerman (1997, p. 5), who surveyed historical trends with regard to the treatment of vocabulary throughout the history of language instruction and SLA,

> the teaching and learning of vocabulary have been undervalued in the field of second language acquisition (SLA) throughout its varying stages and up to the present day. SLA researchers and teachers have typically prioritized syntax and phonology as "more serious candidates for theorizing." (Richards, 1976, p. 77)

Fortunately, increased research on L2 vocabulary over the past two to three decades has increased the ability to approach vocabulary instruction in a manner that is theoretically grounded and supported by more and more concrete research findings related to L2 vocabulary learning.

PURPOSE OF THE BOOK

The purpose of this book is to explain and exemplify an approach to L2 vocabulary instruction that relies heavily on concrete research findings and the theoretical advances that they support. The approach, known as *input-based incremental (IBI) vocabulary instruction,* considers the cognitive and psycholinguistic processes involved in L2 vocabulary learning and, as the name suggests, emphasizes the critical roles of (a) how target vocabulary is presented to learners as *input* (samples of the target language) and (b) how activities can be designed to support the incremental buildup of different aspects of vocabulary knowledge over time. The book provides brief explanations of the theoretical underpinnings of the IBI approach as well as a variety of research findings that support it. It also focuses on how to put the IBI approach into practice on a day-to-day basis and includes many sample IBI lessons and explanations of them. All of the sample lessons are designed for the context of teaching English to speakers of other languages

(TESOL). However, instructors of other L2s can readily adapt the information and sample lessons in the book to create IBI vocabulary lessons for the languages they teach.

Before moving on to the details of IBI approach, the rest of this chapter (a) provides a brief historical perspective on how vocabulary has been addressed in different instructional methods and approaches over time and (b) presents five key questions that instructors of English as a second language (ESL) and English as a foreign language (EFL) and instructors of other L2s might ask themselves regarding their own experience with L2 instruction and possibilities for adjustments in the future. The historical review provides an opportunity for instructors to assess how their own approach to L2 vocabulary instruction compares to other instructional methods and approaches over time and to consider how the IBI vocabulary instruction differs from other trends in vocabulary instruction. The five questions encourage instructors to step back and assess their current practices and possible adjustments when it comes to L2 vocabulary instruction.

A BRIEF HISTORY OF L2 VOCABULARY INSTRUCTION

Zimmerman (1997) discusses how trends in L2 vocabulary instruction have varied greatly over the past two centuries. Under the Grammar Translation Method of the 1800s, students were typically presented with a variety of literary vocabulary to be used for translation, and vocabulary was directly instructed only if a word demonstrated a specific grammatical rule (Kelly, 1969; Zimmerman, 1997). "Bilingual word lists (vocabularies), used as instructional aids rather than as reference, were organized according to semantic fields and had been a normal part of grammars and readers since the mid-seventeenth century" (Zimmerman, 1997, p. 6). Subsequently, in Henry Sweet's Reform Movement, which was developed in opposition to the Grammar Translation Method, speaking and phonetic accuracy, or fluency, were emphasized. Additionally, target words were to be those found in everyday usage and were selected according to their "simplicity and usefulness" (Zimmerman, 1997, p. 8). Following the Direct Method, developed by Sauveur and popularized by Berlitz, vocabulary was selected based on whether it formed part of an "earnest" question for which the instructor was truly interested in an answer and whether the sentences in which the vocabulary appeared provided enough context for learners to deduce the meaning of the vocabulary; such vocabulary was generally "simple and familiar" (Zimmerman, 1997, p. 8).

As Zimmerman (1997) also points out, in the 1920s and 1930s, a period associated with the Reading Method in the United States and Situational Language Teaching in Great Britain, Michael West (from Great Britain) was concerned about which words L2 learners should acquire. He began to focus extensively on the use of word frequency lists to advance the field in this regard, leading to West's (1953) *A General Service List of English Words*, which was based on frequency of word usage in English and could be used for selecting and ordering the English vocabulary that should be learned during the first 3 years of study. West's focus on controlling the level of difficulty of vocabulary at different levels of instruction is also evident in the series of graded readers he developed as part of the New Method system in the 1920s (see Smith, 2007, for an online biography focused on West's life and career). Other British linguists, such as H. Palmer and A. Hornsby, who were working within Situational Language Teaching, believed that vocabulary should be taught via meaningful, situation-based oral activities and through a process of selection, gradation, and presentation of linguistic structures (Richards & Rodgers, 1986). According to Zimmerman, the work of West and Palmer consisted of initial attempts to develop principles of vocabulary control and vocabulary syllabus design.

In the mid-1940s, with the Audio-Lingual Method (ALM), which was developed by structural linguists such as Charles Fries, L2 instruction focused on the idea of resolving a conflict between first language (L1) and L2 linguistic systems by requiring the learner to perform a barrage of oral repetition and substitution drills. From this perspective, vocabulary was viewed as less important than grammar. Words were selected based on their simplicity and familiarity. New words were added as drills progressed but only if the new words did not inhibit drill performance, because it was believed that too many vocabulary words during the early stages of learning would give learners a "false sense of security" about their abilities in the L2 (Zimmerman, 1997, p. 11). Also tied to ALM is the idea that after establishing sufficient control of grammar, one might then move on to a massive expansion of vocabulary (see, e.g., Lado, Baldwin, & Lobo, 1967).

Communicative Language Teaching (CLT), which enjoys widespread popularity today, emphasizes the development of communicative competence, or the ability to communicate effectively by means of a variety of different types of competence—including phonological, lexical, grammatical, pragmatic, and sociocultural. In CLT, learners are exposed to words in the input during meaningful exchanges, and lexical competence develops naturally over time. Krashen and Terrell's (1983) communicatively oriented Natural Approach, for example, allows learners to acquire new words by exposing them to meaning-bearing comprehensible input over time. Decontextualized vocabulary-building activities are not encouraged because they do not promote the type of implicit or incidental acquisition desired. Krashen (1989, 1993) also has argued that advanced L2 learners should engage in free voluntary reading as an effective means of increasing their L2 vocabulary knowledge.

INCIDENTAL AND INTENTIONAL VOCABULARY LEARNING

In addition to the trends described thus far, as the amount of research on L2 vocabulary has risen in recent decades, substantial attention has been given to the roles of incidental and intentional L2 vocabulary learning. *Incidental vocabulary learning* refers to when students learn new words from their context without intending to do so. Two examples of incidental vocabulary learning are learning new words during free reading without intending to do so or picking up new words during a conversation without intending to do so. In contrast to incidental vocabulary learning, *intentional vocabulary learning* refers to situations in which learners actively try to learn new words while intending to do so. Two examples of intentional vocabulary learning are looking at word–picture pairs on a screen and attempting to learn the new words and completing a series of activities in a workbook in an effort to learn a set of target L2 words.

Instructional activities designed to promote incidental vocabulary learning can be referred to as *indirect vocabulary instruction*. In indirect vocabulary instruction (or incidentally oriented vocabulary instruction), an instructor does not explicitly ask students to attempt to learn new words. Instead, the instructor has students engage in certain types of activities, such as reading a text for meaning or completing an information-exchange task, with the understanding that learners may acquire new words incidentally during these types of activities. *Direct vocabulary instruction*, on the other hand, refers to instruction that engages learners in intentional vocabulary learning. It may involve a variety of activities, such as working with a picture file to teach learners new words or workbook activities in which learners are asked to try to learn new words by filling in blank spaces with the words, matching words to their definitions, and so forth.

Many contexts of vocabulary learning are neither purely incidental nor purely intentional, however; they can be viewed on a continuum because attention is not a dichotomous entity (Gass, 1999; Haynes, 1998). For example, an instructor talking to students about various objects in the classroom while focusing on meaning (e.g., *I really like where they placed the windows and the blinds; it allows the room to get a lot of sun.*) may not be a completely incidental context because one or more students may decide intentionally to try to remember a new word (e.g., *blinds*). Reading a text for meaning while paying some additional attention to new words in the text also would not constitute an instance of completely incidental nor completely intentional learning. As another example, a learner may hear a series of new words repeated one by one in a communicatively oriented context while focusing on a particular task, such as checking to see if all of the pieces in a game are present (e.g., *OK, we need the ball, the dice, the cards, the score card. Can you double-check? OK, let's see. Ball? Dice? Cards? Score card? OK, I think we're set.*). The listener may be focusing on the larger task of preparing to play the game, but also paying careful attention to one or more of the new words (e.g., *dice*) being repeated in the process.

Although researchers and instructors alike acknowledge that a vast amount of L2 vocabulary can be learned incidentally, research on incidental L2 learning has led to what many have viewed to be disappointing results. Schmitt (2010, p. 29) notes that "early research on vocabulary acquisition from incidental exposure in reading found a discouragingly low pickup rate" but attributes some of these findings to methodological weaknesses. Other studies have demonstrated that an intentional orientation (simply instructing learners to attempt to learn target words) leads to more vocabulary gains than an incidental orientation (instructing learners to read for meaning without instructing them to attempt to learn specific target words; e.g., Hulstijn, 1992). Findings such as these have led to another, more recent trend in L2 vocabulary instruction: calls for direct L2 vocabulary instruction as a complement to incidental vocabulary learning alone. Nation (2001) argues that this research "underlines the need for training learners in guessing from context and for complementing learning from context with more deliberate vocabulary focused learning" (p. 120). Acknowledging the limitations of relying on incidental vocabulary learning alone, researchers and instructors have brought the need to include direct L2 vocabulary instruction (and intentional L2 vocabulary learning on the part of students) to the forefront.

All of the historical trends in L2 vocabulary instruction described so far suffer from limitations. Some lack empirical support, such as the approaches of early L2 instructional methods and Krashen's (1989, 1993) general call for incidental vocabulary learning through free reading, in light of research findings demonstrating superior vocabulary learning for intentional as compared to incidental orientation (Hulstijn, 1992; see also Barcroft, 2009; Paribakht & Wesche, 1997). Others fail to present a fully developed program for effective L2 instruction, as is the case with many of the calls for more direct L2 vocabulary instruction. What is needed is a more fully developed approach to L2 vocabulary instruction that is theoretically grounded and supported by the expanding body of research afforded by increases in L2 vocabulary research in recent decades. IBI vocabulary instruction was designed to meet these needs. It is a more fully developed approach and is based directly on a variety of recent developments in theory and research on L2 vocabulary learning.

FIVE KEY QUESTIONS ABOUT L2 VOCABULARY INSTRUCTION

Many instructors of ESL/EFL and other L2s are interested in providing effective vocabulary instruction for students but may not be sure of what specific steps to take in order to do so. The multitude of teaching contexts in which instructors find themselves also makes it impossible to provide a one-size-fits-all solution to L2 vocabulary instruction. Whereas one instructor teaches English to Korean high school students in Seoul, another teaches English to Canadian elementary school children of immigrants in Toronto, another teaches private English lessons to university-level students who have traveled to England to complete university studies at Oxford, another teaches English to Spanish-speaking university students in Argentina or any other Latin American country, and so forth. With these examples in mind, let us begin by addressing five key questions that are pertinent to *all* instructors, regardless of teaching context, as they consider how to approach L2 vocabulary instruction on a day-to-day basis:

1. How do you currently teach vocabulary (if at all)?

2. What resources are available to you for teaching vocabulary?

3. What are your current ideas about effective vocabulary learning?

4. Why should you adopt the IBI approach?

5. How can you use IBI vocabulary instruction in your classroom?

1. How do you currently teach vocabulary (if at all)? As noted earlier, the numerous different teaching contexts in which instructors find themselves necessitate a certain degree of flexibility when making adjustments to improve L2 vocabulary instruction. Nevertheless, one thing that all instructors can do is to make an assessment of their own current teaching practices when it comes to vocabulary. How do you currently teach vocabulary? How do you select target words? Are the target words preselected for you based on your use of one or more specific course texts or course readings? How do you present vocabulary to students? What do you do to help ensure that students have remembered target vocabulary over time? How do you test target vocabulary? How do you score vocabulary tests?

Some instructors may assert that they do not really teach vocabulary but instead simply create the conditions in which L2 vocabulary learning can happen. One can contemplate how this approach might be a viable and defendable one. Consider how much vocabulary children learn in this manner when they acquire their L1. They learn vast amounts of vocabulary in this context and typically do so in the absence of any type of formal program of vocabulary instruction. This vocabulary is acquired incidentally and in an incremental manner over time as children listen to and attempt to communicate with other individuals in their environment. If children can learn such a large amount of L1 vocabulary in this manner, why not work to create similar conditions in the classroom for learners to be able to acquire large amounts of L2 vocabulary?

When addressing this question, it is helpful to consider some of the key differences between L1 vocabulary learning among children and the variety of contexts in which L2 vocabulary learning can occur. Children learning their

L1 typically have numerous hours "on task" listening to native speakers of the L1 in question, including consistent exposure to vocabulary. Therefore, even if incidental vocabulary happens slowly or only in spurts (such as during the "fast mapping" stage of L1 vocabulary learning), this context of vocabulary learning allows plenty of time for children to learn hundreds and thousands of words incidentally. Individuals learning L2s often do not enjoy the luxury of such a large amount of time. Many are learning the L2 in a classroom, in a country where the L2 is not spoken as the primary language, or both. Therefore, direct vocabulary instruction and intentional learning may be more appropriate when it comes to those L2 learning contexts, at least for the large number of L2 learners with limited time available and limited exposure to the target L2.

2. What resources are available to you for teaching vocabulary? In addition to defining current teaching practices with regard to vocabulary, it also may be helpful to make an assessment of resources that are available to you for teaching vocabulary. Are the resources for vocabulary instruction primarily tied to the course texts you use? Besides course texts, what other supplementary materials are available to you to facilitate developing effective L2 vocabulary instruction lessons? To what extent do you currently use resources available online? If you do not currently use online resources, what adjustments could you make for them to be more readily available?

Even if your primary resource for teaching vocabulary to date has been only your course text(s), a number of online resources are available to you for selecting target words and addressing other aspects of L2 vocabulary learning. For example, the online Academic Word List (AWL; Coxhead, 2000; www.victoria .ac.nz/lals/resources/academicwordlist) is a list of 570 word families that do not form part of the 2,000 most frequent words in English, which is useful for ESL/EFL students who are beyond the beginning and low-intermediate levels. It was developed for use by ESL/EFL instructors teaching students preparing for tertiary (university-level) study or by students studying vocabulary alone in an attempt to learn vocabulary needed for tertiary-level study. The 5,000-word level of the Vocabulary Levels Test developed by Schmitt, Schmitt, and Clapham (2001; see also Schmitt, 2010) has been described as "perhaps the most widely used vocabulary size test in the ESL/EFL context" (Schmitt, 2010, p. 197). Because the test reflects word frequency in English, including the 5,000-word level, it includes words of substantially low frequency in English and is appropriate for selecting (and testing) target words for higher level learners. The test is copyrighted by Norbert Schmitt, but he has made it freely available for noncommercial research and pedagogical purposes at www.nottingham.ac.uk/~aezweb /research/cral/doku.php?id=people:schmitt#other_output . To access the test, click on the pdf file below the listing of "Schmitt, N., Schmitt, D. and Clapham, C. (2001)" under the heading "Journal Articles" and view the test in the Appendices of the article.

Going beyond individual words, Martinez and Schmitt (2012) also developed a list of the 505 most frequent English phrasal expressions (formulaic sequences such as *money talks* and *on the other hand*), which instructors also now can begin to use to include formulaic language when identifying and working on target vocabulary (for more information on the development of this list, see, e.g., Martinez & Schmitt, 2011). This list, known as the PHRASE List, is available at http://sfsu .academia.edu/RonMartinez/Papers/1335501/A_Phrasal_Expressions_List.

In addition to target vocabulary lists based on frequency, numerous other online lists of L2 vocabulary are available, including field-specific vocabulary such as for business at http://businessvocabulary.org (a website that provides free exercises, videos, and lessons related to finance/banking-related vocabulary) and for health-related fields at www.vocabulary.com. Field-specific vocabulary can be found on a variety of other different websites as well. Another website that may be of use to instructors of ESL/EFL and other L2s is Tom Cobb's Compleat Lexical Tutor (www.lextutor.ca), which offers a number of beneficial features, including the ability to cut and paste English texts to determine information about the relative frequency of the words in the text and a word-associates test. These are just some of the many online resources available to instructors interested in providing students with more effective L2 vocabulary instruction.

3. What are your current ideas about effective vocabulary learning? In addition to making assessments about current teaching practices and available resources, it also can be beneficial to reflect on your own ideas about what conditions and tasks help to promote L2 vocabulary learning in the most effective manner. As human beings, we often have intuitions and maintain world views about the way different phenomena in the world work or should work, including with regard to the effects of specific *learning conditions* (e.g., presenting new words many times as opposed to one time) and *tasks* (e.g., writing new words in sentences, copying new words) on L2 vocabulary learning. Sometimes our intuitions are confirmed when evidence becomes available to support them. Other times they are disconfirmed when evidence becomes available to contradict them. In the latter case, it is important that we reevaluate our intuitions and adopt a new perspective.

When it comes to L2 vocabulary learning, it is fortunate that today we can make use of an increasing body of empirical evidence about the relative effectiveness of different learning conditions and tasks in order to assess and reassess our current ideas about what we think is or should be effective on a fairly regular basis. To explore this issue further, complete Activity 1.1, which asks you to indicate your beliefs about how L2 vocabulary learning is affected by different types of tasks and learning conditions. After you have finished this activity, the rest of the chapter expands on the important role of research in helping explain various processes involved in L2 vocabulary acquisition and improving L2 instruction through the development and implementation of evidence-based practices.

Activity 1.1 Your Current Ideas About Effective L2 Vocabulary Learning

Complete the table below by indicating with an X the effect that you think each of the following tasks and learning conditions would have on learning new words in an L2. Unless otherwise indicated, you may assume that vocabulary learning is *intentional* and that the posttest measures include assessment of the learners' *productive* knowledge of target words (see a picture or L1 translation and try to produce the target L2 word).

Task or Learning Condition	Positive	Negative	No Effect
1. Writing target words in original sentences			
2. Copying individual target words			
3. Answering questions about the meaning of target words			
4. Making pleasantness ratings about the meaning of target words			
5. Counting letters in target words			
6. Making pleasantness ratings as compared to counting letters (Mark "positive" if pleasantness ratings have a more positive effect and "negative" if pleasantness ratings have a more negative effect.)			
7. Generating L1 synonyms for target words while reading a text (*with* explicit instructions to learn the target words)			
8. Generating L1 synonyms for target words while reading a text (*without* explicit instructions to learn the target words)			
9. Presenting eight 3-second repetitions of a target word as compared to presenting two 12-second repetitions of a target word			
10. Allowing learners to generate target words on their own			
11. While holding constant the total time of exposure, gradually increasing the amount of time between presentations of a target word			
12. Presenting target words in an acoustically varied format based on multiple speakers, voice types, or speaking rates			

The findings of various studies on L2 vocabulary acquisition suggest that the answers to Activity 1.1 are as follows. The effect of each task for Numbers 1–8 is *negative* (Barcroft, 1998b, 2000, 2002, 2003b, 2004a, 2006, 2009), whereas the effect of each task or learning condition for Numbers 9–12 is *positive* (Bahrick, Bahrick, Bahrick, & Bahrick, 1993; Barcroft, 1998a, 2007a; Barcroft & Sommers, 2005; McNamara & Healy, 1995; Royer, 1973; Sommers & Barcroft, 2007). To what extent were your ideas consistent with the answers suggested by the research? If at least some of your answers differed from those suggested by the research, the principles and approach to L2 vocabulary presented in this book may help you to view certain aspects of L2 vocabulary acquisition from a different perspective.

Most of the findings referred to in the preceding paragraph are the product of research focused on L2 vocabulary learning from an input-processing perspective. *Input* refers to any sample of the target language to which we are exposed. *Input processing* refers to how we attend to different aspects of the input (e.g., the formal component, the meaning conveyed, grammatical structures) from a cognitive perspective. As will be discussed further in Chapter 2, a substantial number of research findings in this area (on word-level input processing) contradict some commonly held beliefs about the effects of different learning conditions and tasks on L2 vocabulary learning. One common misconception is that elaborating on word meaning (by means of writing words in sentences or addressing questions about word meaning) is a good way to learn words from the start. Another is that copying target words while trying to learn them should be helpful. The origins of these misconceptions and the research that refutes them (e.g., research demonstrating the negative effects of sentence writing, questions about word meaning and word copying on early L2 word learning) are discussed in more depth in Chapter 2.

4. Why should you adopt the IBI approach? IBI vocabulary instruction is an approach that emphasizes the presentation of target vocabulary as *input* early on and the *incremental* (gradual) buildup of different aspects of vocabulary knowledge over time. There are a number of reasons why adopting the IBI approach can work for instructors of ESL/EFL and other L2s in their efforts to provide more effective vocabulary instruction to students. Consider the following five reasons.

First, the IBI approach is based on a theoretical perspective that is consistent with all of the research findings behind the answers to Activity 1.1 and many other research findings. As mentioned earlier, the idea that writing target words in sentences or copying target words produces negative effects on the initial stages of L2 word form learning may be counterintuitive to many, but that is what the research indicates. Therefore, it is better to follow an approach that is designed to be consistent with research findings as opposed to designing activities that studies have demonstrated to be ineffective, or just relying on wishful thinking without considering research at all. Of course, this applies not only to what is ineffective at a particular stage of L2 word learning (e.g., writing target words in sentences, copying words at the early stages of learning a set of new L2 words) but also to what is effective. For example, if immediate L2 word learning increases from 38% to 64% when target words are spoken by six talkers instead of one talker (holding the overall number of repetitions constant), as Barcroft and Sommers (2005) demonstrated, why not make provisions to include more talker variability when presenting target words to students so that they can enjoy the benefits of this type of spoken input? The IBI approach is designed to help students benefit from existing research in this way as much as possible. The more carefully the approach is applied, the greater the benefits.

Second, IBI vocabulary instruction takes learners into account from a cognitive perspective and considers learners' limited processing resources when it comes to L2 vocabulary learning. There are numerous aspects involved in learning a new word. Among these are the word form; all of the word's meanings, including L2-specific meanings and usage that differ from those found in the learner's L1 (e.g., a Spanish-speaking English learner needs to use the phrase *to cash a check* instead of *to change a check,* the latter of which is a literal translation of *to cash a check* [*cambiar un cheque*] in Spanish); and all of the word's various collocations (words that co-occur with a word, e.g., we say *a brief visit* instead of a less natural sounding phrase such as *a quick visit* or *a fast visit* because the sequence *brief + visit* is a collocation). Clearly, a learner cannot be expected to learn all of these aspects of word knowledge at once. What is needed is an approach that encourages a gradual buildup of word knowledge over time, and IBI vocabulary instruction is designed to do just that.

Third, IBI vocabulary lessons are easily incorporated into a variety of instructional contexts. The approach was designed keeping in mind that acquiring English or any other L2 is largely an implicit process that takes place gradually over time as learners attempt to communicate in the target language. Therefore, as will become evident in the various example vocabulary lessons presented in this book, the IBI approach fits seamlessly within an approach to teaching that is largely meaning oriented and that encourages the development of *communicative competence* (e.g., all of the various types of linguistic competences, including sociolinguistic competence) over time through exchange of meaning (e.g., comprehending messages, producing messages) and interaction (e.g., negotiation of meaning, clarification, repair). In other words, the approach fits well into programs that involve "real-world" use of the target language. Additionally, if an instructional program happened to involve many form-focused drills divorced from communicative language use, the incorporation of IBI vocabulary lessons would necessarily bring more communicative language use into the program.

Fourth, IBI vocabulary instruction is designed to promote the development of all aspects of vocabulary knowledge over time, including learning L2-specific meanings and usage, and collocations. As mentioned earlier, numerous aspects are involved in learning any word or lexical phrase, and learners simply cannot learn everything all at once. The IBI approach is designed to respond to this situation by gradually but persistently encouraging learners to build up various aspects of word knowledge over time. What is known and what remains to be learned about a word or a lexical phrase varies according to the background of the learner in question and the extent to which they have been exposed to the target word or lexical phrase in question. As Nation (2001) notes,

> the "learning burden" of a word is the amount of effort required to learn it. Different words have different learning burdens for learners with different language backgrounds and each of the aspects of what it means to know a word can contribute to its learning burden. (p. 23)

The IBI approach is designed to support learners in meeting the learning burden for any target vocabulary by focusing on how the vocabulary is presented as input and pushing learners to build up multiple aspects of vocabulary knowledge in an incremental but thorough manner over time.

Fifth and finally, the IBI approach is designed to incorporate not only current but also future research findings related to L2 vocabulary learning. As will be made clear in Chapter 2, the final principle of IBI vocabulary instruction is to incorporate current and future research findings that have direct implications for L2 vocabulary instruction on an ongoing basis. Instructors following the IBI approach are encouraged to maintain a list of research findings that have direct implications for L2 vocabulary instruction in the classroom, vocabulary-related activities to be completed by students outside of class, or both. One research finding that can be included in this list is the positive effect of having multiple talkers present target words in the input, as mentioned previously. Instructors (and designers of instructional materials) can prepare recorded materials spoken by multiple talkers instead of just one talker when presenting target words in the classroom or in computer-based activities for students outside of class. Another research finding that can be included in the list is the positive effect of background music on L2 vocabulary (de Groot, 2006). Instructors can plan lessons that incorporate background music at the appropriate time so that students benefit from it. The IBI approach encourages maintaining an ongoing list of research findings such as these in order to provide students with the most up-to-date evidence-based approach to L2 vocabulary instruction possible.

5. How can you use IBI vocabulary instruction in your classroom? The best way to incorporate the IBI approach in your classroom is to (a) learn the 10 principles of IBI vocabulary instruction presented in Chapter 2, (b) make use of the seven-item checklist for the design and implementation of IBI activities presented in Chapter 3, and (c) take advantage of the numerous sample lessons presented in the remainder of the book. The 10 principles may include some unfamiliar terms, such as *semantic elaboration* and *forced output without access to meaning,* but these terms are defined and exemplified when the principle in question is explained and discussed in Chapter 2. The seven-item checklist presented in Chapter 3 is designed to be used and reused as needed in order to make sure that the vocabulary lessons that you design continue to be consistent with the basic tenets of the approach, such as presenting target vocabulary in the input first and gradually increasing the difficulty of activities over time. Chapter 3 also includes a sample lesson along with commentary on how the lesson satisfies each of the seven items on the checklist and provides a set of target words that you can use to create your own vocabulary lesson and to assess the extent to which it conforms to the seven items on the checklist. The numerous sample lessons and corresponding commentary in the remaining chapters are designed to demonstrate the IBI approach in action. You can use these lessons as needed to promote learning target vocabulary in your classroom and to gain more experience in how to design and implement IBI vocabulary lessons on your own for any given set of target vocabulary.

CHAPTER 2

Ten Principles of Effective Vocabulary Instruction

The 10 principles of input-based incremental (IBI) vocabulary instruction are as follows:

1. Develop and implement a vocabulary acquisition plan.

2. Present new words frequently and repeatedly in the input.

3. Promote both intentional and incidental vocabulary learning.

4. Use meaning-bearing comprehensible input when presenting new words.

5. Present new words in an enhanced manner.

6. Limit forced output without access to meaning during the initial stages.

7. Limit forced semantic elaboration during the initial stages.

8. Promote learning L2-specific word meanings and usage over time.

9. Progress from less demanding to more demanding activities over time.

10. Apply research findings with direct implications for vocabulary instruction.

In this chapter we discuss each of these principles in turn, including the rationale, research support, and theoretical grounding of each, as appropriate. For quick and easy reference, the 10 principles also appear in Table 2.1. Note that Barcroft (2004c) previously discussed 5 of the principles with reference to a previous shorter version of the IBI approach. Barcroft (2005) also discussed 10 principles of a previous version of the IBI approach while focusing on vocabulary instruction for L2 Spanish. The previous version of Principle 8 was *Respect different stages of the development of vocabulary knowledge,* which is changed to *Promote learning L2-specific word meanings and usage over time* in order to emphasize further the importance of being proactive when it comes to helping learners move through different stages of development, particularly with regard to L2-specific aspects of knowledge and usage.

Note also that the use of the term *words* in Principles 2, 4, and 8 is meant to include words that occur within lexical phrases, including idiomatic expressions

Table 2.1 Ten Principles of Effective Vocabulary Instruction

1.	Develop and implement a vocabulary acquisition plan.
2.	Present new words frequently and repeatedly in the input.
3.	Promote both intentional and incidental vocabulary learning.
4.	Use meaning-bearing comprehensible input when presenting new words.
5.	Present new words in an enhanced manner.
6.	Limit forced output without access to meaning during the initial stages.
7.	Limit forced semantic elaboration during the initial stages.
8.	Promote learning L2-specific word meanings and usage over time.
9.	Progress from less demanding to more demanding activities over time.
10.	Apply research findings with direct implications for vocabulary instruction.

and other types of formulaic language. Each lexical phrase can be considered a single unit in addition to the individual words that make up each lexical phrase.

PRINCIPLE 1: DEVELOP AND IMPLEMENT A VOCABULARY ACQUISITION PLAN

The first principle is to develop and implement a vocabulary acquisition plan within a larger L2 instructional program. Just as planning and implementation are central to a successful L2 instructional program in general, these processes are also important for promoting vocabulary acquisition in an effective manner. One of the advantages of classroom-based foreign language instruction, although it may not involve the constant flow of language input that an immersion experience may offer throughout each entire day, is the opportunity to structure courses and course sequences in a manner that provides learners with level-appropriate goals, materials, and activities over time. This process of planning and implementation commonly begins with the creation and development of textbooks by textbook writers and publishers and then involves selection of a textbook or textbooks; course design, including syllabus design; and development of supplementary materials (in addition to the course textbook) on the part of a language program director, course coordinator, instructor, or some combination of these individuals. With regard to the role of vocabulary in this process, there are two key issues to consider: (a) the selection of target vocabulary and (b) the extent to which vocabulary development will be a focus in light of the need to promote development in other areas of linguistic competence, such as grammar.

In addition to the selection of target words, another important issue is the overall amount of attention that will be paid to vocabulary in the design of a course. As discussed in Chapter 1, from a historical perspective, vocabulary has been undervalued, whereas other areas of linguistic competence, such as grammar, have been prioritized in L2 instruction (Zimmerman, 1997). As our understanding of the central role of vocabulary in knowing a language continues to grow, however, we can adopt alternative approaches that emphasize the acquisition of vocabulary to a much greater degree. In the process of course design, we can question the extent to which we want a course syllabus to be grammatically based versus lexically based. Willis (1990), for example, proposes *The Lexical Syllabus* as a new approach in this regard (cf. Sinclair & Renouf, 1988; see also Lewis, 1993, which introduces the lexical approach, and Lewis, 1997). Willis's approach emphasizes the real-world use of the most frequent words and phrases in language. The lexical syllabus approach has focused substantially on the Collins Birmingham University International Language Database (COBUILD) corpus used to identify different properties of English words, such as word frequency and word collocates. Another available corpus is the Oxford English Corpus. You can explore the Oxford English Corpus (Oxford University Press, 2006) and how it can be used to see collocates of different English words at http://oxforddictionaries.com/words/the-oxford-english-corpus. Whether one chooses to adopt an approach such as the one described by Willis (or Lewis and others) or simply modify existing syllabi to include a greater focus on vocabulary development, emphasizing vocabulary development as a central component of an L2 instructional program is clearly warranted and justified.

An effective vocabulary acquisition plan also should include a theoretically grounded and research-based approach to teaching target words, one that creates conditions that facilitate and promote the acquisition of vocabulary on an ongoing basis. The remaining nine principles provide a framework for developing this type of instruction.

PRINCIPLE 2: PRESENT NEW WORDS FREQUENTLY AND REPEATEDLY IN THE INPUT

As with most areas of language acquisition, without *input* (samples of the target language), vocabulary acquisition simply does not happen. Principle 2 suggests the critical element of presenting new words frequently and repeatedly in the input. Although this principle may seem obvious, at times one can forget the limited extent to which learners are exposed to the target words as input if they are engaging in "other" activities from the onset of being exposed to a word. If students are required to use new words in activities before they have had sufficient opportunities to process them as input, the students may struggle to perform the activities and not learn the target words as well. By allowing students the time and energy they need to process new words as input, teachers can avoid dividing the students' attention and exhausting the processing resources that they need to adequately attend to new word forms. One more traditional option is to provide students with a sufficient amount of time to view translated lists in a textbook, but regular use of this option is not as engaging as including other options, such as using a picture file to present and discuss target words; providing definitions of target words; identifying and labeling real-world items, or *realia* (using real-word items, such as a set of pliers, to demonstrate the meaning of the word *pliers*); using target vocabulary during a discussion on a particular topic; using vocabulary when telling a story; and providing readings that include target vocabulary.

Frequently and repeatedly also is an important component of Principle 2. One very intuitive research finding demonstrated by L2 vocabulary studies is that words presented more often in the input are learned more than words presented less often. Studies such as those by Hulstijn, Hollander, and Greidanus (1996) and Chen and Truscott (2010) have demonstrated this effect for incidentally oriented contexts of L2 vocabulary learning. Barcroft (1998a) also demonstrates the effect for intentional L2 vocabulary when overall time of exposures was held constant: more repetitions at shorter presentation intervals (e.g., eight repetitions at 3 seconds each) produced more L2 vocabulary learning than fewer repetitions at longer intervals (two repetitions at 12 seconds each or four repetitions at 6 seconds each). This finding suggests that when presenting new words in picture files or in other ways, the number of times a target word appears in the input is critical.

Increased repetitions in such contexts need not turn the activity into an entirely rote endeavor, however. An instructor can increase repetitions while still drawing attention to word meaning and to intermittently discussing issues related to the target words in a meaningful and communicative manner. Research by Hulstijn, Hollander, and Greidanus (1996) suggests that increased exposure to target words also can have positive effects in reading-based L2 vocabulary learning. As with many other types of learning curves, the curve for learning new L2 words (and the lexical phrases they form) is driven by increased exposure.

How can we increase the number of times a target word appears in the input without doing so in a rote manner? As the sample lessons in this book demonstrate clearly, target words can be repeated numerous times in the input while maintaining an engaging focus on meaning overall. Consider, for example, a case in which the terms *obstacle* and *obstacle course* are part of the target vocabulary for a lesson. The following segment demonstrates how these terms can be repeated many times in the input while maintaining an overall focus on meaning (related to TV shows about contestants participating in obstacle courses): *I think all of the shows are based on contestants who have to go through <u>obstacle courses</u>. If you know the meaning of the word <u>obstacle</u>—something that gets in your way or blocks your way—you can probably understand what <u>obstacle courses</u> are. To go through an <u>obstacle course</u>, you have to confront and get through different <u>obstacles</u>, like some bar that is spinning around in a circle and somehow you have to jump over it. If you manage to jump over the spinning bar, you go on to the next <u>obstacle</u>, but . . .*

You can see, toward the end of Chapter 3, how this particular segment of input fits a larger IBI vocabulary lesson. It is just one of many demonstrations in this book of how target vocabulary can be presented frequently and repeatedly in the input while maintaining an overall focus on meaning and keeping lessons engaging and interesting.

Principle 2 does not imply always using teacher-led (or teacher-fronted) activities from the start. In the previous example, it is the teacher who presents the target words multiple times, but activities can be designed so that students present target vocabulary to other students, and the direction of communication need not be unidirectional. For example, each student in a class might be (a) assigned to one particular target vocabulary item, (b) provided with written materials that allow each student to process her or his vocabulary item as input and learn it sufficiently well, and (c) asked to prepare a presentation of the item in question for the rest of the class. The guidelines for the activity can clarify that each student must say his or her vocabulary item multiple times (e.g., at least three times) when presenting. To prepare the presentation of the different words, each student can be given a sheet or card that demonstrates clearly the meaning(s) of the target vocabulary item in question (via definitions, examples, visuals, etc.). The sheet or card serves as input for one student first, and then the student provides input for the rest of the class. Presenting target vocabulary in this way is definitely not teacher fronted, helping to support the goal of a balance between the amount of teacher-fronted and non–teacher-fronted activities in the classroom. Additionally, whether target vocabulary is being presented as input by students or by the teacher, the act of doing so can be quite interactive, involving questions for others and allowing for negotiation of meaning, comprehension checks, and a variety of modified input (e.g., rephrasing a sentence until it is understood) along the way.

Principle 2 also does not imply that students should not engage in extensive independent reading and listening. In contexts of extensive free reading and listening, there may be many opportunities for learners to pick up target words from context. Other IBI principles can be applied to these more independent contexts of learning, such as Principle 3, which involves engaging learners in both intentional and incidental vocabulary learning. A learner may engage more intentional learning mechanisms if asked to attempt to learn any new words or expressions in an extended reading (or listening) and to rely solely on incidental vocabulary learning when reading (or listening). This and other principles with implications for varying free reading (and listening) are discussed more extensively in Chapter 5.

PRINCIPLE 3: PROMOTE BOTH INTENTIONAL AND INCIDENTAL VOCABULARY LEARNING

Because vocabulary can be learned in both intentionally oriented and incidentally oriented contexts, instructors can take advantage of both opportunities as much as possible. Additionally, as discussed in Chapter 1, the lines between purely intentional versus incidental vocabulary are blurred by the range of activities that fall between the endpoints of the incidental–intentional continuum, and all points on the continuum have a place in promoting as much L2 vocabulary learning as possible over time.

Interestingly, the presentation of target words as isolated items also has an important role in first language (L1) vocabulary learning with children. Research on caregiver speech indicates that the presentation of isolated words (words presented alone and not in the context of a sentence) is a reliable characteristic of the input that children receive when learning their L1. Brent and Siskind (2001) found that, on average, approximately 9% of infant-directed utterances are isolated words. Therefore, repetition of isolated words in meaningful contexts may be important in L1 vocabulary learning; isolated words may help to make words more salient and easier to learn, and learners may decide to make intentional attempts to attend to and learn (more intentionally) words that are presented in this manner. In light of this situation, it makes sense to include isolated lexical items as part of the input during L2 learning so that L2 learners, like L1 learners, also can take advantage of the beneficial properties of this type of input.

The decision about which L2 words should be taught more directly (intentional learning) and which words should be taught more indirectly (incidental learning) can be a part of the planning discussed with regard to Principle 1. For learners at lower levels of L2 proficiency, more direct vocabulary instruction can help them to reach thresholds of word knowledge that will allow them to acquire more new words from context. Nation and Waring (1997) calculated that with a vocabulary of the 2,000 most frequently used words in English, one can reach an English text comprehension level of about 80%, which corresponds to approximately 1 out of 5 words being unknown. They also argued, however, that learners need to know approximately 3,000 words of high frequency in a language and that these words should be of high priority in an immediate sense.

Whatever threshold level one selects as a goal, it is more likely that one will reach that level using a combination of direct and indirect instruction as opposed to relying on indirect instruction (and incidental learning) alone. Nagy, Anderson, and Herman (1987) calculated that the probability of learning a new word from context is only between 5% and 20%. The 5% figure was used to calculate that, upon reading a million words in 1 year, children can learn 1,000 words per year (Nagy et al., 1987; see also Nagy, 1997; Nation & Waring, 1997)—not a particularly encouraging figure. However, simply instructing learners to attempt to learn new words in a text (and telling them that they will be tested on the words) can substantially increase vocabulary learning during reading (e.g., Barcroft, 2009; Hulstijn, 1992; see also Paribakht & Wesche, 1997). Additionally, the use of direct methods (intentional learning) to complement L2 vocabulary learning is another viable and effective method. Paribakht and Wesche (1997), for example, found that combining direct instruction with incidentally oriented instruction was more effective at promoting L2 vocabulary learning than incidentally oriented instruction alone.

For learners at higher levels of L2 proficiency, one may wish to rely more on incidental vocabulary learning but include more direct vocabulary learning instruction (intentional learning) to promote the acquisition of less frequent or field-specific target words (e.g., words related to medicine, engineering, botany) to which the learners may not be exposed on a regular basis. Advanced-level learners do not always reach the levels of competence that their teachers might like by relying on incidental vocabulary alone. Arnaud and Savignon (1997) demonstrated that this is the case when it comes to learners' command of idiomatic expressions. Therefore, it may be quite useful to use direct instruction (and intentional learning) with advanced-level L2 learners to ensure more learning of idioms, field-specific vocabulary, and other areas of vocabulary in which even these learners have room for improvement.

When creating more intentionally oriented vocabulary activities, it may be helpful to use tools available online, such as Hot Potatoes (http://hotpot.uvic .ca), freeware that has six applications that enable teachers to create various kinds of interactive online exercises. After learners have had sufficient opportunities to process target vocabulary as input, online activities such as these may help them consolidate the vocabulary, and these activities can be assigned for learners to complete outside of class, allowing more class time for other communicatively oriented interactive activities.

PRINCIPLE 4: USE MEANING-BEARING COMPREHENSIBLE INPUT WHEN PRESENTING NEW WORDS

This principle is a central tenet of the IBI approach. Without sufficient activation of meaning, learners have no way of mapping L2 word forms onto their meanings. This perspective is consistent with Krashen's (1985) view of second language acquisition (SLA) in general and with other perspectives that view language acquisition as a long-term and consistent process of form–meaning mapping. According to Krashen, meaning-bearing comprehensible input is a necessary ingredient for successful SLA, and the construct of $i + 1$, or input slightly above one's current level of competence, is the key ingredient for gradually increasing one's level of competence in the target language. The $i + 1$ construct also may be applied to the process of vocabulary acquisition. If input is largely incomprehensible, a learner is less likely to infer the meaning of a new word, as compared to input that is completely comprehensible with the exception of one individual new word or lexical phrase.

Examples of this can be seen in sentence-level input providing definitions of words. Compare the following two definitions: Definition 1: *A cork is a porous material of arboreal origin adapted to encase and prevent leakage of mellifluous material.* Definition 2: *A cork is what we use to cover bottles to keep water, wine, and other liquids inside.* If an L2 learner of English does not yet know the meaning of *cork* intended to be explained in each of these two definitions, Definition 2 is more likely than Definition 1 to help the learner understand because Definition 2 is most likely going to be more comprehensible to the learner and provide her or him with better opportunities for making a new form–meaning connection for the word form *cork* and, at least, one of its meanings.

Principle 4 is also consistent with proposals made by Nation (2001), who argues that a balanced language course should include four strands: (1) meaning-focused input, (2) language-focused learning, (3) meaning-focused output, and (4) fluency development (p. 401). Nation notes that conditions for learning within the strand of meaning-focused input include *focus on the message, include a small number of unfamiliar items* (which appears to be consistent with Krashen's notion of *i* + 1, at least in principle), and *draw attention to new items.* Example activities that Nation mentions for meaning-focused input include extensive graded reading, listening to stories, and working with familiar content. The latter two are included among the various other examples of meaning-bearing input in sample lessons presented in this book.

Once provisions have been made to ensure that the input presented to learners is going to be meaning bearing, what are some techniques that can be used to make the meaning-bearing input more comprehensible?

- Speak clearly and at a slower pace.

- Use more gestures and paraphrasing.

- Repeat sentences and individual words.

- Use shorter sentences, and pronounce individual target words at a particularly slow pace.

- Provide a variety of examples.

- Use different types of comprehension checks, such as yes/no questions, to ensure that learners are understanding (see, e.g., Hatch, 1983).

Techniques such as these help to render input more comprehensible and in this manner provide more opportunities for learners to attend to new L2 word forms and attach meaning to them. Because vocabulary is the place where form meets meaning at a very basic level, even the presentation of word-picture (or even translation) pairs on cards can be considered meaning-bearing input. Upon deciding to involve cards of this sort as a means of presenting target words as input, one may wish to consult Mondria and Mondria-De Vries (1994), who provide suggestions on how to do so efficiently. See also Nakata's (2011) comprehensive analysis of nine flashcard programs based on 17 criteria.

One of the benefits of using sentence- and discourse-level input when presenting target vocabulary is that this type of input helps to promote *chunking*—the mental grouping of items (such as words) that tend to co-occur in a language—and increased sensitivity to the statistical properties inherent in the target language in question. Consider differences in the use of *make* and *do* in English, for example. By processing sufficient sentence-level input over time, L2 learners come to learn that *you do your homework and may make a mistake* (but never the other way around, at least in English). Also, *part of doing the housework is making your bed* (but again, not the other way around). This type of knowledge about collocation (how words do and do not co-occur with other words) is a critical part of not only vocabulary learning but also language learning in general. How this type of knowledge develops over time is a central issue in connectionist (emergentist) theoretical approaches to language learning. These approaches emphasize the gradual buildup of associative knowledge related to collocations in such a way that learners and language users become sensitive to various types of frequency-related properties inherent in the target language in question (see, e.g., Ellis, 2006, for discussion and examples of these issues in an article on the Associative-Cognitive CREED, which asserts that SLA is construction-based, rational, exemplar-driven, emergent, and dialectic). Without meaning-bearing and (sufficiently) comprehensible input at a level that goes beyond individual words and other types of vocabulary items, the learner has no basis on which to develop this type of knowledge.

PRINCIPLE 5: PRESENT NEW WORDS IN AN ENHANCED MANNER

Input enhancement refers to techniques for making input more salient in an attempt to draw learners' attention to these features (Sharwood Smith, 1991; see also Wong, 2005). Research on input enhancement for L2 grammar instruction has produced mixed results, but some findings suggest that different types of input enhancement (including textual enhancement) can increase learners' noticing and intake with regard to grammatical structures (see Wong, 2005, for a review). Hulstijn and colleagues (1996) found that enhancement in the form of including definitions of words in marginal glosses had positive effects on L2 vocabulary learning during reading. Additionally, Barcroft (2003a) found that textually enhancing target words by bolding them and increasing font size had positive effects on intentional L2 vocabulary learning, provided that the enhancement was sufficiently distinctive. Scores for enhanced words were higher if 3 out of 24 target words (in a list of L2 words with their L1 translations) were textu-ally enhanced (Experiment 2) but not if 9 out of 24 target words were textually enhanced.

These findings suggest that input enhancement may improve learners' ability to attend to and learn target words, at least under some conditions. Some of the techniques that L2 instructors may wish to try are underlining target words, bold-ing them, and putting them in capital letters. Using electronic formats, one can explore more elaborate varieties of enhancement, such as having words appear in different colors, having words flash on the screen, or even having words move around the screen. Although techniques such as these may not be tested to date with regard to their effects on learning new L2 words, based on past research it seems reasonable to hypothesize that they might help learners attend to target L2 word forms and in this way, at least potentially, learn the words at least somewhat more readily. Additionally, Barcroft and Sommers (2005) and Sommers and Bar-croft (2007) demonstrated that L2 vocabulary learning is substantially improved when target words are presented using multiple talkers, speaking styles (voice types), or speaking rates. Acoustically varied input of this nature may extend a bit beyond modifications traditionally associated with input enhancement (and for this reason is discussed more at length with regard to Principle 10: Apply research findings with direct implications for vocabulary instruction), but its effectiveness has been well demonstrated. For example, as mentioned in Chapter 1, Barcroft and Sommers (2005) found that having six speakers present six tokens of target words resulted in a 64% level of more vocabulary learning, as compared to 38% when all six tokens were spoken by one talker.

PRINCIPLE 6: LIMIT FORCED OUTPUT WITHOUT ACCESS TO MEANING DURING THE INITIAL STAGES

Principles 6 and 7 are based directly on research findings revealing negative effects of certain types of semantically elaborative and forced-output tasks. Prin-ciple 6, which suggests limiting forced output without access to meaning (see Lee & VanPatten, 2003, on the distinction between output *with* versus *without* access to meaning) during the initial stages of L2 vocabulary learning, is supported by the findings of a study on word copying by Barcroft (2006). In this study, English-speaking second-semester learners of Spanish attempted to learn 24 new words by viewing word–picture pairs on a screen at the front of the class. For 12 of the words, they copied each word each time they saw it (word writing). This is a form of *output without access to meaning*, which refers to repeating what one hears in a "parroting" manner instead of attempting to retrieve and produce a target word or phrase on one's own. For the other 12 words, the participants wrote nothing. The results of both experiments indicate that productive vocabulary scores were significantly lower in the word-writing conditions, based on both immediate and delayed (2 days later) posttests. Overall means (collapsing immediate delayed measures) were 4.95 for no writing versus 3.71 for word writing in Experiment 1 and 5.77 for no writing versus 4.77 for word writing in Experiment 2.

There are two important implications of this study (cf. Thomas & Dieter, 1987; see Barcroft, 2006, for discussion of differences between this study and Thomas and Dieter's study, which found positive effects for writing practice under certain conditions). First, the findings provide evidence that word writing can exhaust processing resources that learners otherwise could have allocated toward processing new words as input. Second, the findings suggest that some, but not all, of the observed negative effects of sentence writing (see discussion for Principle 7) on L2 vocabulary may be attributed to forced output in the form of writing.

The *without access to meaning* component of this principle is crucial because giving learners opportunities to attempt to generate target words on their own after they have had opportunities to process the target words as input positively affects L2 vocabulary learning. Studies by Royer (1973), McNamara and Healy (1995), and Barcroft (2007a) demonstrate that having learners retrieve target words or giving them opportunities to do so after they have had an opportunity to process the words as input positively affects novel word learning (note that by nature one cannot retrieve a new word that one has not been exposed to in the input). These findings are consistent with the *generation effect* in psychological research on human memory (Slamecka & Graf, 1978), which refers to the observation that memory for an item is better when an individual is required to generate (or attempt to generate) the item based only on a cue.

When creating and implementing activities designed to promote L2 word learning, instructors should identify whether the type of output elicited from students (if any) during the early stages of learning the target words will involve output *without* access to meaning (as in the case of copying target words while attempting to learn them) or *with* access to meaning (as in the case of retrieving target words on one's own). Research findings suggest that only output with access to meaning is going to have a positive effect. In order for learners to produce this type of output, they first must be given an opportunity to process target words as input, as advocated by the IBI approach.

PRINCIPLE 7: LIMIT FORCED SEMANTIC ELABORATION DURING THE INITIAL STAGES

The seventh principle of IBI vocabulary instruction is to limit forced semantic elaboration during the initial stages of L2 word learning. *Semantic elaboration* refers to a situation in which one is focused more on aspects of the meaning of a word than would otherwise be the case. An example of semantic elaboration would be if one considers the extent to which the word *snail* represents an example of an animal, an insect, a food, or another category. An example of *structural elaboration*, on the other hand, would be if one counts the number of letters or syllables in the word *snail* or thinks of words that rhyme with it. Principle 7 is based on the predictions of the *type of processing–resource allocation* (TOPRA) model (Barcroft, 2000, 2002) and the findings of studies on the negative effects that have been observed for tasks such as sentence writing, answering questions about word meaning, and making pleasantness ratings on the early stages of L2 word form learning.

The TOPRA model (Barcroft, 2000, 2002, 2003b) was designed to represent visually how different types of processing can produce different types of learning outcomes. Three versions of the model appear in Figure 2.1. In each version, the thick outer lines remain stable because they represent the restricted amount of processing resources available to a learner. The inside lines can move, however, as different types of processing and corresponding types of learning increase or decrease, the basic idea being that each type of processing must exhaust processing resources. As one type of processing increases due to a specific type of task demand, others must decrease to accommodate. The amount and type of learning that ultimately takes place will reflect this kind of trade-off (see Barcroft, 2002, for discussion of TOPRA in light of levels of processing [Craik & Lockhart, 1972] and transfer-appropriate processing [Morris, Bransford, & Franks, 1977]).

The TOPRA model can be used to focus on how different types of processing should affect learning rates for distinct components of word knowledge, such as word form, word meaning, and form–meaning mapping. Whereas Version A (see Figure 2.1) is the general version of the model, Version B focuses on processing for word meaning, word form, and form–meaning mapping, and Version C focuses specifically on the semantic and formal components of word learning for contexts in which these two components are in play. Version C demonstrates most clearly the prediction that (when processing demands are sufficiently high) increased semantic processing can increase learning for the semantic (and conceptual) properties of words while decreasing learning for their formal properties. Word form learning decreases under these conditions because fewer processing resources remain available to process for word form.

Barcroft (1998b, 2000, 2004a) provided initial support for the TOPRA model by demonstrating that semantic elaboration in the form of sentence writing negatively affects L2 word form learning. In the study, English-speaking learners of Spanish attempted to learn 24 new Spanish words while writing 12 of them in original sentences versus viewing the other 12 words as input only. The results indicated that productive vocabulary learning was much better on both immediate and delayed measures when learners were not required to write the target words in sentences. Figure 2.2 depicts the negative effects of sentence writing in one of the experiments (from Barcroft, 2004a) on both immediate and delayed (2 days later) measures of productive vocabulary learning over time. In a more recent study, Wong and Pyun (2012) also demonstrated strong negative effects of sentence writing for learning vocabulary in L2 French and Korean (see also Folse, 2006, for a demonstration of how sentence writing fared poorly when compared to other techniques of direct vocabulary instruction).

A. General Version: Types of Processing and Learning

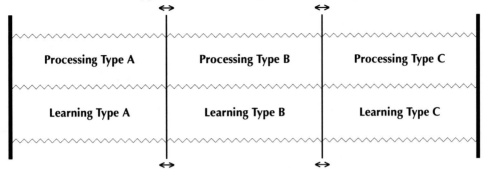

B. Components of Vocabulary Learning: Semantic, Formal, and Mapping

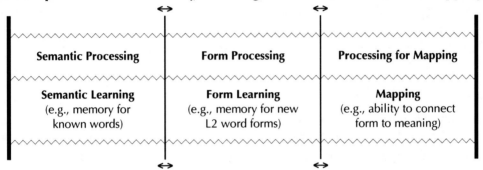

C. Semantic and Formal Components of Vocabulary Learning

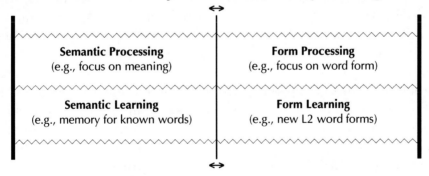

Figure 2.1 Type of Processing–Resource Allocation (TOPRA) Model

These findings are consistent with those of another study by Barcroft (2006) in which English-speaking learners of Spanish attempted to learn 24 new Spanish words. For 12 of the words, they were asked to answer specific questions in their mind related to the meaning of each target word, such as *In what ways can this object be used?* For the other 12 words, they were instructed only to do their best to learn the target words and were not asked to answer questions. Productive L2

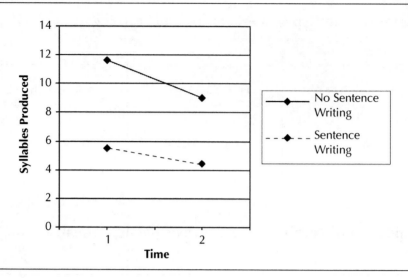

Figure 2.2 Negative Effects of Sentence Writing on L2 Vocabulary Learning

vocabulary learning (in this case, *see a picture, attempt to produce the target L2 word*) was significantly lower in the no-questions condition as compared to the questions condition. These findings provide further evidence for the TOPRA model by demonstrating another negative effect of another semantically elaborative task during early L2 word learning.

In another study that tested the predictions of the TOPRA model, Barcroft (2002) compared the effects of a semantically oriented task, a structurally oriented task, and a control condition on L2 vocabulary learning among English-speaking learners of Spanish. All of the participants were asked to do their best to learn 24 new Spanish words while viewing word–picture pairs on a screen. For one group of 8 words, the participants were required to make pleasantness ratings about the meaning of target L2 words based on their prior experience while attempting to learn the words. This task was semantically oriented. For another group of 8 words, they were required to count the number of letters in the words while attempting to learn the words. This task was structurally oriented. Finally, for another group of 8 words, they were asked only to do their best to learn the target words and were not required to perform any additional task. After the learning phase, the participants performed three posttest tasks. First, they were asked to do a free recall of the target words in Spanish. In a *free recall* task, participants simply try to remember words to which they have been exposed, in this case by writing them and numbering them on a blank sheet of paper. Second, the participants were asked to do a free recall task of the words in English. Third, they were asked to do a picture-to-Spanish cued recall task. *Cued recall* refers to when one is asked to recall something based on the presentation of another item as a stimulus, in this case a picture of the referent of each target Spanish word.

Before considering the findings of the study, let us review what predictions the TOPRA model would make for each of the three learning conditions. First, it would predict that the semantically oriented task would increase processing and learning for the formal aspects of the overall task but decrease processing and learning for aspects that are dependent on semantically oriented learning or memory. Given that the Spanish free recall and the picture-to-Spanish cued recall were largely dependent on how well the participants had learned the new word forms, the TOPRA model would predict higher Spanish free recall for the structural (letter counting) as compared to the semantic (pleasantness ratings) task. Given that the English free recall was not dependent on learning new word forms (because the participants already were English speakers) and more dependent on semantically oriented memory (being able to activate the meaning of the words in one's mind in order to recall it), the TOPRA model would predict higher English free recall for the semantic task as compared to the structural task.

The results of the study were consistent with the predictions of the TOPRA model. Spanish free recall scores were higher for the letter-counting (+structural) task than for the pleasantness-ratings (+semantic) task, but English free recall was higher for the pleasantness-ratings (+semantic) task than for the letter-counting (+structural) task. These findings, which are depicted in Figure 2.3, are predicted by the TOPRA model. The increased semantic processing invoked by the +semantic task decreased processing resources that otherwise could have been allocated toward encoding the new L2 word forms. The results of the study also indicate that Spanish cued recall, which is also dependent on learning new L2 word forms, was not higher for the +semantic task as compared to the +structural task. Based on one scoring method sensitive to partial knowledge of target word forms, L2 word learning means were 1.58 for the +semantic task versus 1.96 for the +structural task, but this difference did not reach a level of statistical significance ($p = .089$). Clearly, the semantically elaborative task was of little benefit to learning the new L2 word forms as compared to the other conditions.

Are negative effects of semantically oriented tasks on early L2 word learning limited to contexts of intentional L2 vocabulary learning only, or, alternatively, might the increased semantic processing that they invoke help learners attend to target words more readily in less intentional, more incidentally oriented contexts of L2 vocabulary learning? Barcroft (2009) addressed this question and tested the generalizability of the TOPRA model with regard to intentional and incidental vocabulary learning during reading. In this study, Spanish-speaking learners of English at low-intermediate and high-intermediate levels read an English passage containing 10 new English words translated in the text. Increased semantic processing was operationalized by requiring participants to generate L1 (Spanish) synonyms for target words. Four conditions were examined: read for meaning;

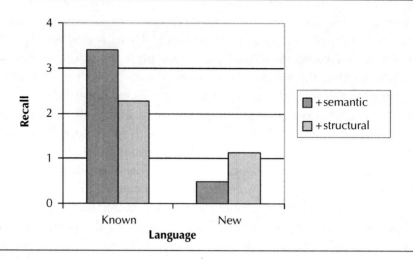

Figure 2.3 Effects of Making Pleasantness Ratings (+semantic) Versus Letter Counting (+structural) on Free Recall

read for meaning and generate Spanish synonyms for the translated words; read for meaning and attempt to learn the translated words; and read for meaning, attempt to learn the translated words, and generate Spanish synonyms for these words. Vocabulary learning was assessed based on scores on two types of posttests: Spanish-to-English and English-to-Spanish translation. Passage comprehension also was assessed based on a short-answer test. Independent variables were condition (incidental, explicit), task (–synonym, +synonym), level (low-intermediate, high-intermediate), and recall type (Spanish-to-English, English-to-Spanish). Vocabulary score and comprehension score were dependent variables.

The results of the study indicated that vocabulary learning scores were significantly higher for the explicit over incidental condition and significantly lower when participants were required to generate synonyms. The negative effects of synonym generation appeared in both the explicit and incidental conditions with no significant interaction between condition and task. These results are depicted in Figure 2.4. These findings provide additional support for the TOPRA model and suggest that its predictions about the potential negative effects of semantically oriented tasks can extend to both intentional and more incidentally oriented contexts of vocabulary learning. As also depicted in Figure 2.4, vocabulary learning scores were significantly higher in the intentional conditions as compared to the incidentally oriented conditions in the study. Explicitly instructing learners to attempt to learn new words (which were translated in this case) in a passage had a positive effect on the extent to which they learned those words, regardless of whether they were asked to perform the semantically oriented synonym-generation task as well.

Note that Laufer and Hulstijn's (2001) *involvement load* hypothesis, which has

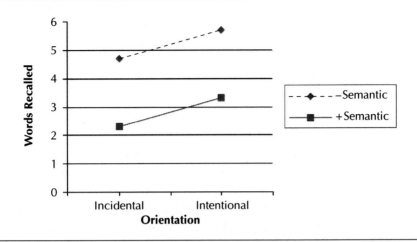

Figure 2.4 Negative Effects of L1 Synonym Generation (+semantic) on Incidental and Intentional L2 Vocabulary Learning During Reading

provoked substantial interest among L2 vocabulary researchers, predicts that semantically oriented evaluation is one factor (in addition to need and search) that positively affects incidental L2 vocabulary learning. *Evaluation* in this context concerns "a comparison of a given word with its other meanings, or combining the word with other words in order to assess whether a word (i.e., a form–meaning pair) does or does not fit its context" (Laufer & Hulstijn, 2001, p. 14). Hulstijn and Laufer (2001) tested the predictions of the involvement load hypothesis by comparing the effects of three learning tasks on L2 English learners' retention of the meaning of 10 English words. They created an involvement index to classify the three tasks with regard to the factors of need, search, and evaluation: (1) reading comprehension with marginal glosses received an involvement index of 1 because it was deemed to induce moderate need but no search or evaluation; (2) reading comprehension plus a fill-in-the-gap task received an involvement index of 2 because it was deemed to induce moderate need, no search, and moderate evaluation; (3) writing a composition and incorporating target words received an involvement index of 3 because it was deemed to induce moderate need, no search, and strong evaluation. Immediate and delayed retention post-tests focused on word meaning were administered. The results indicated higher retention for the composition task than for the other two tasks.

The researchers interpreted these results as support for the involvement load hypothesis. However, time on task was not held constant for each of the three conditions. Time on task was reported to be at about 40–45 minutes for reading with glosses (the task associated with the lowest retention), 50–55 minutes for fill-in-the-gap (the task associated with the second highest retention), and 70–80 minutes for composition (the task associated with the highest retention), making the results very difficult to interpret when it comes to learning efficiency. Putting aside this problem (and others, such as lack of precision when it comes to isolating some types of cognitive processes from others during activities such as gap fill or composition writing), it is important to understand that the involvement load hypothesis and the posttests designed to test it focus on word meaning primarily, whereas the TOPRA model makes predictions about the relationship between both meaning and form.

The findings of the studies reviewed in this section weigh heavily against the idea of requiring learners to elaborate excessively on aspects related to the meaning of target words during the early stages of trying to learn them because this type of elaboration can detract from their ability to attend to and learn target word forms. If any type of semantic elaboration is to be done during the initial stages of learning a new word, it would be most useful if it concerns L2-specific meanings of target words so as not to be redundant with what learners already know about the meaning of words based on their L1 experience. For example, if the target word in question is *kettle,* asking learners to remember the last time they used a kettle or what type of kettles they prefer to use to cook is not going to help them learn the word form *kettle* and, in fact, can get in their way of doing so; therefore it would be an ineffective task when it comes to learning the word form. If the elaboration is directed toward the meaning of the idiom *the pot calling the kettle black,* however, this type of elaboration, assuming the L1 of the learner does not include this exact expression, is likely to be more useful because the learner's L1 counterpart for *kettle* is not used in this manner.

PRINCIPLE 8: PROMOTE LEARNING L2-SPECIFIC WORD MEANINGS AND USAGE OVER TIME

The eighth principle concerns different stages of development in vocabulary knowledge and, in particular, how students learn the form and meanings of words and lexical phrases in bits and pieces over time. Whereas Principles 6 and 7 suggest avoiding output without access to meaning and semantically elaborative activities during the early stages of learning a new L2 word, Principle 8 suggests that meaning-oriented activities focused on L2-specific meanings and usage of words (and not on redundant L1–L2 overlap in meaning), are needed to develop more complete knowledge of target vocabulary. Recall from the discussion of Principle 4 how presenting words as meaning-bearing and (sufficiently) comprehensible input at the level of sentences and discourse helps learners develop critical frequency-sensitive knowledge about word meanings and collocations. Principle 8 is consistent with this idea but also with the idea of "going further" than Principle 4 alone by designing activities that target L2-specific meanings and usage that may not have appeared in the input or may not have become apparent to learners based on the provision of target words in the input up to any particular point in time.

Consider Bogaards's (2001) work on the notion of *lexical unit* when it comes to L2 vocabulary learning. According to Cruse (1986), a lexical unit is "the union of a lexical form and a single sense" (p. 77). Bogaards argues that this term should be utilized in the realm of L2 vocabulary learning. A *monosemic* word (a word with one meaning) and the sense that it conveys can be considered as a single lexical unit. Bogaards lists *necessarily, hotpot,* and *ruche* as examples of lexical units of this nature (p. 326). Lexical units can also be composed of lexical phrases that contain more than one word as well, such as the idiom *the pot calling the kettle black,* as mentioned previously. Other examples listed by Bogaards are *pull a fast one, hot dog,* and *flag day* (p. 326).

What is important then, as Principle 8 suggests, is that L2 learners have opportunities to learn all of the various lexical units connected to target words and lexical phrases (beyond those they have learned based on provision of meaning-bearing and sufficiently comprehensible input [Principle 4] up to a given point in time), particularly when the lexical units in question diverge from what the L2 learners have learned in their L1. Bogaards (2001, p. 324) provides a good example by demonstrating five distinct senses (five lexical units) for the English word form *party*:

1. *Our neighbors are throwing a party tonight.*

2. *They were very grateful to the rescue party.*

3. *The Conservative Party has lost many votes.*

4. *The lawyer refuted the arguments of the other party.*

5. *Your party is on the line.*

The long-term goal is for learners to be able to acquire all of these senses and thereby have command over the five different lexical units in question. In an English as a second or foreign language (ESL/EFL) classroom with students who all share the same L1, it may be possible to determine which of these lexical units are connected to one word form in the learners' L1 (e.g., Example A corresponds to the Italian word *festa,* whereas Example C corresponds to *Partito*) in order to determine where there is and is not redundancy, but oftentimes ESL/EFL classrooms are composed of students with a variety of L1s. In such cases, it may be necessary to cover all of the various senses of any given word or lexical phrase. This can be done either by directly teaching the distinct meanings or through less direct means, but it is a critical part of helping learners achieve an increasingly more complete command of the target vocabulary. It can be beneficial to point out shared meaning in all of the different senses of a word as well. In the case of *party,* for example, it may be useful to note how the various senses in Examples B through D have an underlying shared meaning of "group."

Knowing the Idioms

Because individual words are also used in combination, knowing the idioms in which a given word appears is ultimately part of knowing the L2-specific meaning and usage of that word. Such a requirement may seem like setting a very high bar for word knowledge, but that is part of the essence of Principle 8. Why not set the bar high? If one has learned standard meanings of *casa* ("house") and *ventana* ("window") in Spanish, that is good, but consider the additional value of knowing that in Spanish you can "throw the house out the window" (*tirar/echar la casa por la ventana*) when throwing a party or planning an event and expense is no matter. Similarly, in English, knowing the basic meanings of the words *roll*, *red*, and *carpet* is certainly good but not as good as also being able to tell others when it is (and is not) time to *roll out the red carpet* when planning a party or some other type of event. Clearly, the more knowledge one is able to develop with regard to the use of words in different idiomatic expressions, the more fully developed one's knowledge of the words is going to be, in addition to the fact that every idiom in a language is a potential target vocabulary item as a unit in and of itself (without denying separable compositional features, such as use of metaphor, inherent in idioms).

Explicit instruction and learning of idioms can be enjoyable and beneficial to language learning. Explaining the meaning of an idiom, providing information about its origin, or both constitute meaning-bearing input (cf. Principle 4). In designing and implementing lessons that focus on idioms, instructors can gain insights from previous research in this area. As Boers (e.g., 2001) has demonstrated, increasing learners' awareness about the metaphoric nature of idioms, such as by asking them to supply possible origins of different types of figurative idioms such as *pass the baton* and *run someone ragged*, can have a positive effect on learning idioms (see also Boers, Eyckmans, & Stengers, 2007, on the benefits of providing information about the etymology of idioms, such as for *white elephant* when referring to a gift that imposes a financial burden: "The rare albino elephant was much prized by the kings of Siam. Keeping it was very costly, and so it was likely to ruin any courtier to whom the king gave it as a gift" (p. 61). Boers (2001) explains how different dimensions may contribute to the benefit in different ways: Overarching metaphoric themes provide an organizational framework (for the figurative dimension in which idioms work) that is easier to learn; for example, if *the body is a container for emotions* and *anger is heat*, then expressions like *she was fuming*, *I was boiling with anger*, *simmer down*, and *she flipped her lid* among others (examples from Boers, 2001, p. 35) can be viewed as being related. Boers also points out that interest in this approach to idioms is linked to the impact of cognitive semantic theory (e.g., Lakoff, 1987; Lakoff & Johnson, 1980; see Boers, 2011, for more on the cognitive linguistics approach to L2 vocabulary learning and a review of research in this area; see also Boers & Lindstromberg, 2009)—and its emphasis on the living conceptual metaphors that underlie figurative idioms—in the field of applied linguistics.

It is important to note that predictions of the TOPRA model regarding specificity in different task types and learning outcomes do not disappear when moving from learning individual words to learning idioms. Recall that from the TOPRA perspective semantically oriented tasks promote learning properties related to the meaning of vocabulary (words, idioms, or otherwise) but are not as well suited for learning word form and, in fact, can negatively impact learning word form when overall processing and learning demands are sufficiently high. Research on how learning the meaning and forms of idioms is affected by the use of pictures to demonstrate the meaning of idioms, or *pictorial elucidation* (a provision directed toward the meaning and not the form of target vocabulary), is consistent with these predictions. In one study, for example, Boers, Piquer Píriz, Stengers, and Eyckmans (2009) assessed whether the benefits of pictorial elucidation on understanding and remembering the meaning of idioms (see the same study for a review) would extend to learning the form of idioms based on a gap-fill test. Assessing learning the form of idioms implies additional complications beyond those involved in assessing learning the forms of individual words (e.g., learners may have prior knowledge of some but not all of the words in any given idiom), but the findings of the study were consistent with TOPRA predictions: "The addition of pictorial elucidation contributes little to learners' retention of linguistic form. Distraction by pictures may even have a detrimental effect when it comes to retaining unfamiliar and difficult words" (p. 367).

Formulaic Sequences

In addition to idiomatic expressions, other types of formulaic language can differ between L1 and L2. Formulaic sequences are phrasal expressions that "behave much the same way as individual words, matching a single meaning or function to a form, although that form consists of multiple orthographic or phonological words" (Martinez & Schmitt, 2012, p. 1). Sometimes formulaic sequences can be similar in L1 and L2, as in the case of the Spanish phrase *tal como* ("such as") and the English phrase *such as*, which in their literal translations are composed of the same individual words. But often L1 and L2 versions of formulaic expressions are composed of different words in varying degrees. For example, the Spanish phrase *de vez en cuando* means "from time to time" but translates literally in English as "from time in when." Processing a sufficient amount of meaning-bearing input in L2 (Principle 4) can help learners greatly in this regard, but particular attention can be given to L2-specific patterns in formulaic usage as part of instruction. As mentioned briefly in Chapter 1, Martinez and Schmitt (2012) have developed a list of the 505 most frequent nontransparent multiword phrases in English (the PHRASE List, available at http://sfsu.academia.edu/RonMartinez /Papers/1335501/A_Phrasal_Expressions_List), which instructors can use to help students develop better knowledge of formulaic patterns in English. In order to determine the degree to which these phrasal expressions do and do not overlap with a learner's L1 and focus instruction on the phrasal expressions that are likely to be more challenging, an instructor would need to have sufficient knowledge of the L1 in question.

PRINCIPLE 9: PROGRESS FROM LESS DEMANDING TO MORE DEMANDING ACTIVITIES OVER TIME

The ninth principle concerns the natural progression of activities in which L2 learners should be engaged over time. It suggests progressing from less demanding to more demanding activities in order to allow learners to build word knowledge in an appropriate and incremental manner. In order for learners to attend to target L2 word forms during the early stages, Principles 6 and 7 suggest avoiding activities that involve output without access to meaning and semantically elaborative activities, particularly those that focus on the semantic overlap between L1- and L2-appropriate meanings and uses of the words in question. After learners have had sufficient opportunities to encode the target word forms in question and make initial form–meaning mappings, activities can be designed to help them acquire L2-appropriate semantic space for target words and be able to produce the target words in an increasingly fluent manner, including with regard to appropriate collocations for the target word in question. In other words, the question is not one of *whether* to include output-inclusive and semantically elaborative activities but *when* to include them, in consideration of learners' developmental stages with regard to different aspects of word knowledge.

The extent to which learners are asked to produce output can gradually increase over time as well. The ultimate goal is for learners to be able to use the target vocabulary in question as adeptly as possible, and producing output in an increasingly fluent manner is part of this goal. Because fluency development is essential for vocabulary growth, Principle 9 is critical. Vocabulary lessons designed according to IBI principles in no way need to be excessively easy; they simply keep the learning burden that learners face in mind at different stages in the lesson. During the early stages, learners face the challenge of learning novel lexical forms (both words and lexical phrases) and need to be allowed to process these forms as input and connect them to their meanings. At this stage it is particularly important "not to get in the learners' way" as they go about processing the target vocabulary as input. At later stages, however, it is important to continue to push learners to learn all of the various meanings and usage of the target vocabulary, particularly those that are distinct from meanings and usage patterns in the learners' L1, and to create conditions that allow learners to produce the target vocabulary in an increasingly fluent manner in different communicative contexts. Fluency development in this manner is a critical aspect of vocabulary development in any language.

PRINCIPLE 10: APPLY RESEARCH FINDINGS WITH DIRECT IMPLICATIONS FOR VOCABULARY INSTRUCTION

This final principle complements the other nine principles of IBI vocabulary instruction by providing instructors and language program developers with opportunities to create a list of research findings with direct instructional implications, to update this list on an ongoing basis as new research continues to appear, and to incorporate the research findings when designing L2 vocabulary lessons.

Chapter 1 introduced some research findings that can be included in this list, such as the finding of positive effects for opportunities to generate target words (Barcroft, 2007a; McNamara & Healy, 1995; Royer, 1973) and increasing the amount of talker, voice-type, and speaking-rate variability when presenting new L2 words as input (Barcroft & Sommers, 2005; Sommers & Barcroft, 2007). Table 2.2 includes other research findings with direct implications for L2 vocabulary instruction. The IBI approach advocates incorporating these and

Table 2.2 Research With Direct Implications for L2 Vocabulary Instruction

Study	Implication
Barcroft (2007a); McNamara and Healy (1995); Royer (1973)	Provide learners with opportunities to attempt to generate target words on their own.
Barcroft and Sommers (2005)	Increase talker variability and voice-type variability when presenting target words in spoken input.
Finkbeiner and Nicol (2003); Tinkham (1997)	Use thematically based (*frog, green, hop, pond, slippery, croak*) and not semantically based (*eye, nose, ear, mouth, chin*) sets of target words (examples from Tinkham, 1997).
Sommers and Barcroft (2007)	Increase speaking-rate variability when presenting target words in spoken input.
de Groot (2006)	Include background music when presenting target words.
Bahrick, Bahrick, Bahrick, and Bahrick (1993)	Gradually increase the amount of time between presentations of a target word over time.
Barcroft (2009); Hulstijn (1992)	Explicitly instruct learners to attempt to learn new words prior to reading.
Hulstijn, Hollander, and Greidanus (1996); Rott (1999)	Increase the number of times target words appear in a text.
Luppescu and Day (1993); Hulstijn et al. (1996)	Allow learners to use bilingual dictionaries during reading.
Hulstijn et al. (1996)	Provide the meaning of words in marginal glosses.
Yun (2010)	Use multiple hypertext glosses in computerized texts.

other findings with direct implications of this nature. The key principles of the IBI approach, particularly those that advocate the presentation of target vocabulary in the input first and instruction that respects and supports the incremental nature of vocabulary learning, are evidence-based principles that apply to basically all cases of L2 vocabulary instruction. But the list maintained for Principle 10 allows instructors to apply other directly applicable research findings when feasible in light of the target vocabulary in question and the context in which it is being taught.

CHAPTER 3

Checklist for Designing and Implementing Vocabulary Lessons

This chapter presents a checklist for designing and implementing effective vocabulary instruction lessons. The checklist, which appears in Figure 3.1, can be copied and used on a repeated basis as needed. It provides instructors with a good way to make sure that they are not forgetting any of the key elements of the input-based incremental (IBI) approach as they work to design and implement effective second language (L2) vocabulary lessons.

The rest of this chapter discusses the rationale for attending to each of the seven items in the checklist. At the end of the chapter, I demonstrate how the checklist can be helpful when attempting to design effective English L2 vocabulary lessons, including assessing the extent to which a lesson conforms to the IBI principles discussed in Chapter 2 and the seven-item checklist discussed in this chapter.

1. I DECIDED ON TARGET VOCABULARY AND MATERIALS NEEDED FOR THE ACTIVITIES

When defining the target vocabulary, each word and lexical phrase may be defined clearly from the start. Other vocabulary may arise as the various activities in the lesson are implemented, but it is good to have a clear idea of the minimum

---

☐ 1. I decided on target vocabulary and materials needed for the activities.

☐ 2. I designed the activities to be meaningful, educational, and interactive.

☐ 3. I included cultural and historical information when appropriate.

☐ 4. I made sure target vocabulary is presented repeatedly in the input first.

☐ 5. I increased the difficulty of tasks involving target vocabulary gradually over time.

☐ 6. I incorporated a number of the principles of the IBI approach.

☐ 7. I included directly applicable research findings.

Figure 3.1 Checklist for IBI Vocabulary Instruction Lessons

set of target vocabulary. If an instructor is working with a list of vocabulary from a textbook, that list can be used. As described in Chapter 1, numerous online sources are also available for selecting target vocabulary.

With regard to materials, it should be clear from the description of the various steps in the lesson what materials will be needed to implement the lesson. Keeping Principle 4 in mind, there is a wide variety of ways to present target vocabulary so that its meaning is comprehended. Instructors can use resources such as *realia* (real-world items), computer presentation programs with pictures, a picture file with pictures on cards, flash cards with target words and definitions (in a variety of different formats), videos, maps, among others. Prerecorded spoken input also can be used in the classroom along with other materials. Instructors can be as creative as they wish in their use of various materials to support the lesson.

2. I DESIGNED THE ACTIVITIES TO BE MEANINGFUL, EDUCATIONAL, AND INTERACTIVE

The second and third guidelines suggest making the activities meaningful, educational, and interactive and including cultural and historical information when appropriate. Not every language learning activity need focus extensively on cultural or historical information, but IBI vocabulary lessons lend themselves well to incorporating such information and, by their nature, consistently involve the interpretation and negotiation of meaning. Even if an activity within a lesson involves defining target words or showing pictures that represent them, this activity is still inherently meaningful because it provides learners with an opportunity to make new form–meaning connections.

3. I INCLUDED CULTURAL AND HISTORICAL INFORMATION WHEN APPROPRIATE

For English language learners, activities can be designed to focus on historical and cultural issues throughout the English-speaking world, but they need not stop there. Similarly, for learners of other L2s, IBI lessons can be designed to focus on historical and cultural issues relevant to the regions where the L2 is spoken as well as outside of those regions. Decisions about which historical and cultural issues to focus on may need to be made in consideration of the larger goals for the particular course being taught. The IBI approach is adaptable to the content of basically any course. It is flexible when it comes to content but consistent when it comes to promoting the buildup of vocabulary knowledge over time based on cognitive considerations related to the L2 learner and what is needed to acquire target vocabulary in an effective manner over time.

4. I MADE SURE TARGET VOCABULARY IS PRESENTED REPEATEDLY IN THE INPUT FIRST

This item stems from a view of vocabulary acquisition that considers the importance of input and input processing. If learners are not exposed to target words in the input, there is no way that they can learn the words. Well-designed IBI activities involve a variety of ways of presenting target words as input, well beyond simply having learners study translated lists of vocabulary. Although providing first language (L1) translations may be appropriate on some occasions, other techniques for presenting target words in the input may provide more opportunities for developing direct form–meaning connections between L2 word forms and their referents. The following are some of the many options available: using a picture file to present and discuss target words, providing definitions of target words, identifying and labeling realia, engaging learners in *total physical response* activities (see, e.g., Asher, 1982) that involve target vocabulary, using target vocabulary during a discussion on a particular topic, using vocabulary when telling a story, and providing readings that include target vocabulary.

5. I INCREASED THE DIFFICULTY OF TASKS INVOLVING THE TARGET VOCABULARY GRADUALLY OVER TIME

The fifth item on the checklist is a critical one because it concerns the *incremental* aspect of the overall approach. IBI vocabulary lessons typically involve a series of activities that build upon one another and that are connected in some way to a central topic, such as doing errands on Saturday morning in Bangkok, going for a walk and having an appetizer before dinner in Italy, or exploring the life and legacy of King Louis XIV. Although topics may vary widely, in each set of activities, the goal is to present the target vocabulary as input before requiring learners to produce the vocabulary or work with it in more demanding tasks. In other words, there should always be one or more activities in which learners are given opportunities to process target words as input and other activities that gradually increase in difficulty with regard to what they require learners to do with the target words. Frequent and repeated presentation of target words in the input should typically occur in the first couple of steps in a lesson, but additional presentations of target words in the input is very beneficial at later stages as well. What is critical is that the difficulty of tasks be minimized during the initial steps because learners need to use a substantial amount of their energy to process target words as input at that stage. Later on, it is important that activities push learners in a way that encourages them to develop more complete knowledge of the target vocabulary and to be able to use the target vocabulary in an increasingly fluent and effective manner when communicating with others.

6. I INCORPORATED A NUMBER OF THE PRINCIPLES OF THE IBI APPROACH

The sixth item in the checklist is a reminder to incorporate many of the 10 principles of IBI vocabulary instruction. These principles are the foundation of the approach. The sample lesson presented toward the end of this chapter includes commentary that clarifies how specific principles can be incorporated. A set of target words also is provided for you to design a lesson on your own. Once you have had sufficient practice designing IBI activities, the process of incorporating principles in new lessons should become increasingly natural, but it can be helpful to reassess whether more principles can be incorporated for any particular lesson.

7. I INCLUDED DIRECTLY APPLICABLE RESEARCH FINDINGS

The seventh and final item on the checklist emphasizes incorporating many directly applicable research findings related to L2 vocabulary learning, as Principle 10 also suggests. Chapter 2 outlined some research findings of this nature (in Table 2.2), including the following:

- the positive effects of giving learners opportunities to attempt to generate target words on their own (Barcroft, 2007a; McNamara & Healy, 1995; Royer, 1973)

- the positive effects of talker variability and voice-type variability (Barcroft & Sommers, 2005)

- the negative effects of presenting words in semantically based sets (Finkbeiner & Nicol, 2003; Tinkham, 1997)

- the positive effects of speaking-rate variability (Sommers & Barcroft, 2007)

- the positive effects of background music on L2 vocabulary learning (de Groot, 2006)

- the positive effects of gradually increasing the amount of time between presentations of a target word (Bahrick et al., 1993)

Other findings focus more on vocabulary learning during reading and are addressed in Chapter 5. In general terms, Principle 10 and this item of the checklist call for an ongoing consideration of the L2 vocabulary research literature in order to be able to expand on the present list of research findings that are directly applicable to the design and implementation of IBI activities or, for that matter, any set of activities designed to promote vocabulary learning.

The rest of this chapter presents a sample IBI vocabulary lesson along with commentary on how it incorporates IBI principles and attends to each item on the checklist, a set of target words that you can use to design a sample vocabulary lesson of your own, and some general comments about the set of target words and how to approach using them to design a lesson.

SAMPLE LESSON

What Do You Think of Obstacle Course Television Shows Like *Wipe Out*?

Target Words: *concussion, contorted, foam, helmet, instant replay, obstacle, obstacle course, padded, ratings, the sky is the limit, to crash, to get knocked off, to get soaked, to injure, to spin, to splash, to wipe out, tube, wet suit*

Step 1. Discuss what obstacle course shows are, and ask students if they have seen them before, what they think of them in general, and names of different shows. When any new target vocabulary is introduced, define it clearly as part of the discussion. For example: *The other day I was watching this show called* Wipe Out *on TV.* Wipe out *is the term that surfers use to describe when they fall in the water, but the people on the show, the contestants,* wipe out *in a lot of different ways. I read online that there are British, Australian, and American versions of this show. They're all called* Wipe Out. *I think all of the shows are based on contestants who have to go through* obstacle courses. *If you know the meaning of the word* obstacle*—something that gets in your way or blocks your way— you can probably understand what* obstacle courses *are. To go through an* obstacle course, *you have to confront and get through different* obstacles, *like some bar that is* spinning *around [gesture "spinning"] in a circle and somehow you have to jump over it. If you manage to jump over the* spinning *bar, you go on to the next* obstacle, *but if not, you typically* get knocked off *and fall into some body of water and* get soaked. *What fun, no?! Have any of you seen these types of shows? What do you think of them?* Continue the discussion until all target words have been presented and defined.

Step 2. Show pictures (at the front of the class) that depict segments of the show or are related to the show in order to depict and reuse all of the target vocabulary. For example: *This next picture really makes me cringe. This guy crashes into a* padded spinning bar, *gets knocked off into the water,* gets completely soaked, *and you can see that his* helmet *kind of starts to fall off when he splashes into the water. I really question whether he was* injured *in this scene. I know that he has a* helmet, *that the bar is* padded, *and that he falls into water as opposed to hitting the ground, but when you* crash *or* wipe out *like this, I just think that it is pretty easy* to get injured. *What do you think?*

Step 3. Tell students that you are going to review vocabulary related to the topic before doing some other related activities. Give each student a sheet of paper with a matching quiz on Side 1 and a "production" quiz on Side 2. Have students complete Side 1 first. To do so, they should draw lines to match target vocabulary with definitions. After students have completed Side 1, go over it as a class and provide the answers. Then have students turn the sheet over. On Side 2, students read definitions of the target words and attempt to write the form of each target word on their own. After all students have completed Side 2, go over it as a class. Do not grade the quiz.

Step 4. Ask students to work in pairs to discuss whether they have seen obstacle course shows in their own country or anywhere else and what they think of them. Also ask them to try to describe one of the obstacle courses they have seen, if they have seen any, and to try to discern whether there are any differences between the obstacle course shows that are shown in different countries.

Step 5. Have a class discussion about obstacle course shows in different countries. Write on the board any new vocabulary that comes up during the discussion, and explain the terms to the students. Ask them to give their opinions about what the obstacle course shows have to say about society today and any cultural differences related to how the shows are enacted in different countries. Note that in Japan there is an obstacle course show called *Sasuke*. Ask if any students have seen this show and how it might be different from the various versions of *Wipe Out* in the English-speaking world. After the discussion has finished, tell students that in the next class they will have a graded quiz on the target words that they practiced in the other quiz today (from Step 3).

Step 6. At the beginning of the next class, administer the quiz to the class (only the Side 2 version from Step 3 in which they have to produce the target word forms).

Step 7. In groups of three, ask students to design an obstacle course with five different obstacles. Each group should explain their obstacle course to the rest of the class. As new vocabulary arises, write it on the board and define it.

Step 8. Show a list of the target vocabulary at the front of the class and initiate a discussion about alternative meanings and usage of the target words and phrases. Many of the alternative meanings that arise may be specific to English and not shared in the students' L1(s). For example: *Consider the term* <u>wipe out</u>. *This can mean* <u>to crash</u>, *but we also can say that the hard drive on a computer was* <u>wiped out</u> *by a computer virus. In other words, the virus destroyed the hard drive.* <u>To spin</u> *means literally to move around in a circular motion, but in politics* <u>to spin</u> *can mean to try to put a good face on something. For example, if a politician does something wrong, supporters of the politician may try* <u>to put a spin on it</u> *or just* <u>spin it</u> *so that it doesn't seem so bad.*

Commentary

This sample lesson demonstrates how target vocabulary can be presented in the input in a repeated manner while focusing the larger discussion on meaning. Steps 1 and 2 provide good examples of this for the target vocabulary *obstacle course* and *to wipe out*. All items in the checklist can be checked for this lesson as well. Consider the following with regard to the seven items on the checklist:

✔ **1. I decided on target vocabulary and materials needed for the activities.** The target vocabulary is defined at the beginning. In this case the target words and phrases lend themselves well to focusing on the topic selected. The materials needed are defined in the steps: pictures of scenes from *Wipe Out*, a way to present them at the front of the class, and a blackboard.

✔ **2. I designed the activities to be meaningful, educational, and interactive.** The topic should be of interest to students, and the activities are clearly interactive because they ask for student opinions, small-group work, and creativity on the part of the students (with the design of the obstacle course in Step 7).

✔ **3. I included cultural and historical information when appropriate.** The rise of obstacle course shows in itself is of interest with regard to the history of television, and the lesson is designed so that students will consider cultural differences related to how such shows are instantiated in different countries. Step 5 addresses these issues directly and even includes specific mention of an obstacle course show in a non-English-speaking country—the show *Sasuke* in Japan.

✔ **4. I made sure target vocabulary is presented repeatedly in the input first.** Steps 1 and 2 clearly demonstrate this item. Although the sample input provided does not tackle all of the target words, following the sample should lead to at least more than one repetition of each target word during the first two steps of the lesson.

✔ **5. I increased the difficulty of tasks involving target vocabulary gradually over time.** Imagine the difficulty that students might experience in working with the target vocabulary had Step 7 come first in this lesson. This would have violated Principle 7 of the IBI approach. Instead, the activities were designed to begin with the presentation of the target vocabulary as input in a manner that allows learners to process the target word forms and their meanings first before being asked to do more with the words. Then, gradually, they are asked to do more over time, leading up to a final activity that requires them to be creative and produce a substantial amount of output (with access to meaning).

✔ **6. I incorporated a number of the principles of the IBI approach.** This lesson is consistent with the principles of the IBI approach. It is both input based and incremental. It is meaning oriented from the beginning but gradually increases demands on the learners in terms of semantic elaboration and output, respecting the learning burden that students face as well as their limited processing resources. Students cannot do everything all at once when it comes to the target vocabulary, but by the end of the lesson they should be able to do much more because the lesson has been designed to help them increase their vocabulary knowledge in an incremental manner. Whereas one might think Step 4 is not consistent with Principle 7 regarding limiting semantic elaboration during the early stages, note that this step comes after learners have numerous opportunities to process the target words as input. It is not that semantic elaboration should never take place; it is that if it takes place too soon, it can detract from word form learning. Step 8 also demonstrates an initial effort to focus on an expanded number of L2-specfic meanings and usage.

✔ **7. I included directly applicable research findings.** One directly applicable research finding incorporated in this lesson is the positive effect of providing learners with opportunities to retrieve target words. If it is possible to include video with audio segments that have other individuals (besides the instructor) producing some or all of the target vocabulary, this would incorporate another directly applicable research finding: the positive effects of talker variability on vocabulary learning.

CREATE YOUR OWN VOCABULARY LESSON

Now that you have read the sample lesson and related commentary, try to create your own IBI lesson, making sure that you can check off all of the seven items on the checklist discussed in this chapter.

Target Words: *apron, charcoal, grill, knob, laid back, mosquito net, playground, rare, side dish, teeter totter, to be a hit, to billow (smoke), to burn to a crisp, to drizzle, to season, to sizzle, tongs, toppings, utensils, well done*

Guidelines for Your Vocabulary Lesson

1. Select a title for the lesson.

2. Include seven to nine steps for the lesson. Write them on a separate sheet of paper.

3. Complete the checklist discussed in this chapter, and if you feel that one item needs to be attended to further at any point, go back and modify the lesson so as to incorporate that item more.

4. Write a commentary for the lesson explaining how you addressed each item in the checklist in designing the lesson.

A Few Points to Consider About Your Vocabulary Lesson

Clearly, the particular set of vocabulary at hand lends itself well to a theme related to grilling or a group picnic of some sort, although not all of the target vocabulary is from the same semantic set, which could lead to confusion and less effective L2 vocabulary learning (Finkbeiner & Nicol, 2003; Tinkham, 1997). Pictures, video, or a combination of both could be a good way to present the target vocabulary in the input during the initial steps of the lesson. The topic of grilling and picnics can be addressed from a variety of historical and cultural perspectives as well. For example, is grilling more common in some countries than others? If so, in which countries is it more popular, and why? How is grilling different in different countries of the English-speaking world, such as the United Kingdom, Australia, the United States, and Canada?

In addition to considerations about the content of the lesson, carefully applying the checklist should ensure that the lesson follows the key principles of the IBI approach, including repeated presentation of the vocabulary as input during the early stages and the incremental buildup of vocabulary knowledge over time, including meanings and usage of the vocabulary in English that may differ from those of learners' L1(s). A step can be included to address alternative meanings of the target vocabulary directly, such as explaining the difference between the use of *to drizzle* when referring to the weather (*It is drizzling out*) as opposed to when it is used with a direct object (*He drizzled syrup on the waffle*).

Finally, if the topic of grilling or picnics is selected, it may work well to design the lesson so that it builds up to a group or all-class activity. After the target words have been learned and the topic has been discussed sufficiently, you may ask students to work together to plan a group picnic or an afternoon of grilling, including details such as when and where it would take place, all of the items that they would need, and different activities that they would want to plan (volleyball, another sport, etc.). Activities of this nature should help students improve their ability to use the target vocabulary in a more fluent and natural manner.

CHAPTER 4

Lessons for Your Classroom, Part I: Using Multiple Sources of Input

The five lessons presented in this chapter depict input-based incremental (IBI) vocabulary instruction in action. They demonstrate how instructors of English as a second or foreign language (ESL/EFL) can present target words using multiple sources of input and assist students in learning a variety of target word sets in an incremental manner. Each lesson is explained in a step-by-step manner and is accompanied by a commentary section with observations about how it incorporates specific aspects of the IBI approach. Instructors can incorporate each of the five lessons in their classroom to promote the acquisition of 100 useful target English words.

SELECTION OF TARGET WORDS FROM THE ACADEMIC WORD LIST AND OTHER SOURCES

As discussed in Chapter 1, ESL/EFL instructors have a variety of resources at their disposal for selecting target words in a systematic and effective manner. The selection of target words for the five lessons in this chapter involved several of these resources. The specific resource used for each lesson is indicated in the following sections.

Note also that for all of these lessons, the lists from which the target words were selected included a number of other words. That is, the words selected for each lesson were only a subset of the larger lists. For example, the words selected for Lesson 1 are from Sublist 5 of the AWL. Sublist 5 includes a total of 60 head-words corresponding to 60 word families, but only 20 of these were selected as target words for Lesson 1.

Lessons 1 and 2

The target words for the first two lessons were selected using the Academic Word List (AWL; Coxhead, 2000). Recall that the AWL includes 570 word families that do not form part of the 2,000 most frequent words in English. It was developed for use by ESL/EFL instructors teaching students preparing for tertiary (university-level) study or by students studying vocabulary alone in an attempt to learn vocabulary needed for tertiary-level study. The entire AWL is available at www.victoria.ac.nz/lals/resources/academicwordlist.

Information about the 10 sublists of the AWL can be found at www.victoria .ac.nz/lals/resources/academicwordlist/thesublists.aspx. The 20 words in Lesson 1 of this chapter were taken from Sublist 5, whereas the 20 words for Lesson 2 were taken from Sublist 10. These two sublists were selected because they demonstrate two different levels of difficulty of the AWL sublists while maintaining a sufficiently high level of difficulty so as to be of use to a wide variety of ESL/EFL students, including students whose L1s share cognates with many of the target words in Sublists 1–4 (as would be the case with students who are native speakers of a Romance language and other Indoeuropean languages).

Lesson 3

The target words for Lesson 3 were taken from the 5,000-word level of the Vocabulary Levels Test developed by Schmitt, Schmitt, and Clapham (2001; in this case from the version of the test that appears in Schmitt, 2010). As discussed in Chapter 1, this test has been described as "perhaps the most widely used vocabulary size test in the ESL/EFL context" (Schmitt, 2010, p. 197). It reflects word frequency in English, and the 5,000-word level includes words of substantially low frequency in English, which are more appropriate for higher level learners than for learners low-intermediate or beginner levels. The test is copyrighted by Norbert Schmitt, but he has made it freely available for noncommercial research and pedagogical purposes (Schmitt, 2010, p. 279). A PDF of Schmitt and colleagues' article appears along with other articles on Norbert Schmitt's website at www .nottingham.ac.uk/~aezweb/research/cral/doku.php?id=people:schmitt.

Lesson 4

The target words for Lessons 4 and 5 represent field-specific vocabulary. The target words for Lesson 4, which focuses on finance/banking-related vocabulary, were taken from the list of Financial-Banking and Accounting Terminology at http://businessvocabulary.org, a website that provides free exercises, videos, and lessons related to finance/banking-related vocabulary.

Lesson 5

The target words for Lesson 5, which focuses on health-related vocabulary, were taken from the Health, Fitness, and Nutrition list at www.vocabulary.com /lists/25156.

SELECTION OF LESSON TOPICS

As discussed in Chapter 1, lesson topics can be selected when one considers a particular set of target words, or a particular set of target words can be selected when one considers a lesson topic to be covered. Topics for Lessons 1–3 were selected by the former method, and topics for Lessons 4 and 5 were selected by using a combination of both methods. For Lessons 1–3, the topics were selected by considering the range of vocabulary in the list in question. The list consulted for Lesson 1 included the words *academy, capacity, generate, network,* and *psychology,* which gave rise to the idea of research on memory and learning as a topic. The list consulted for Lesson 2 included the words *enormous* and *collapse,* which gave rise to the idea of a topic related to the effects of hurricanes and what can be done to deal with hurricanes in the future. The list consulted for Lesson 3 included the words *pail, apron, mess, compliment, tile,* and *tub,* which gave rise to the idea of house cleaning as a topic.

However, the target words are not only lists of semantically related words. They gave rise to different ideas for topics, which is very different from preparing lists of semantically related words. This point is important when one considers the negative effects that have been observed for presenting semantically related as opposed to thematically related target words (Finkbeiner & Nicol, 2003).

The topics for Lessons 4 and 5 were selected to a substantial degree prior to selecting the specific target vocabulary given that the lessons were to focus on field-specific vocabulary from the outset. Lesson 4 was to focus on financial/banking-related vocabulary, and Lesson 5 was to focus on health-related vocabulary. Therefore, field-specific lists were consulted, but more specific topics within the larger field-specific area were selected in consideration of the particular vocabulary lists consulted. This process led to selecting the topics of, for Lesson 4, home loans and refinancing after the most recent housing crisis and, for Lesson 5, ideas about how to stay in good physical shape.

Additionally, when selecting target words for each lesson, an attempt was made to include words from a variety of word classes (not only nouns but also verbs, adjectives, and conjunctions, for example) even though the ability to include a variety of word classes is constrained by the word list being used for target word selection (AWL Sublist 5, AWL Sublist 10, and the other lists). During each lesson, a particular target word, such as the noun *appraisal,* can be used to demonstrate the form and use of other target words in the same word family, such as the verb *to appraise.* The lessons in this chapter use multiple variants of words in a single word family in this manner.

INCORPORATION OF IBI PRINCIPLES IN THE LESSONS: AN OVERVIEW

The key principles that should be most apparent in each of the following lessons are those defined by the name of the IBI approach, namely, that each lesson be input based and incremental. By *input based*, we mean that target words should be presented as input during the earlier stages of learning (i.e., during the earlier steps in the series of steps that constitute each lesson). By *incremental*, we mean that the activities should be presented in an incremental manner such as by giving students sufficient opportunity to learn the new forms during the initial stages (or the earlier steps within each lesson) without requiring them to engage in too much semantic elaboration (additional focus on the meaning-related aspects of words) at that time. Other principles that should be apparent in the lessons are the frequent and repeated presentation of target words, the inclusion of a variety of intentional vocabulary learning activities (along with opportunities for incidental vocabulary learning opportunities, such as when students are exposed to and may use other nontarget words as part of an activity within a lesson), the consistent use of meaning-bearing comprehensible input when presenting target words (via definitions, visuals, etc.), and a general progression from less demanding to more demanding activities over time.

Some lessons also demonstrate enhancement of target words in the input and the incorporation of research findings with direct implications for vocabulary instruction. These cases are pointed out in the commentary section following the lessons in question.

LESSON 1

What Variables Improve Memory and Learning?

Target Words: *academy, adjust, aware, capacity, decline, expand, expose, facilitate, generate, logic, network, orient, perspective, psychology, reject, stable, substitute, sustain, target, whereas*

(Words taken from AWL Sublist 5; Coxhead, 2000)

Step 1. Tell students that you will be having a discussion about research on the effects of different variables on memory and learning and that you will be using 20 target vocabulary words to facilitate the discussion. Ask students to listen to the target words. Pronounce each target word very slowly and clearly, and give students time to hear each word: *academy . . . adjust . . . aware . . . capacity . . .* and so forth.

Step 2. Tell students to listen to the definitions and examples of each word, and then provide definitions for the primary meanings of each target word along with examples that include other members of the word family. Repeat each word after its definition. For example: <u>*Academy*</u> *refers to a place where we study, such as in a university or in a specialized field. University students are in the academy. They are* <u>*academics*</u>*. They have* <u>*academic*</u> *discussions and use* <u>*academic*</u> *vocabulary. That's the meaning of* <u>*academy*</u>. Allow students to ask questions as needed during the explanation of each word.

Step 3. Ask students to take out a sheet of paper, write down each of the target words as you say it, and try to remember the meaning of the word (but they write down only the word). Number and pronounce each target word clearly, for example, *Number 1 is academy. Academy. Number 2 is adjust. Adjust.* And so forth. After students have had an opportunity to attempt to write all of the words correctly, write the target words on the board or present them on a screen at the front of the class so that students can check their spelling. Ask them to cross out any incorrectly spelled words and rewrite them.

Step 4. On a screen at the front of the class (using a computer presentation program, for example) present a list of 20 definitions for the 20 target words in a random order other than the order used to present the words and their definitions in Step 1. Provide students with a blank sheet with the numbers 1–20 on it, and ask them to try to remember and write the correct target word for each definition.

Step 5. Tell students to add five new numbers somewhere in the sheet that they were given. Ask them to listen to four statements that you will be making about research on memory and learning and to indicate whether they think each statement is true or false by writing T or F after each number. Say each of the following four statements out loud two times:

1. <u>*Psychological*</u> *studies on memory and learning indicate that allowing individuals to* <u>*generate*</u> *words on their own (after they are* <u>*exposed*</u> *to them)* <u>*facilitates*</u> *memory.*

2. *According to one theoretical* <u>*perspective,*</u> <u>*orienting*</u> *attention toward the semantic (meaning-related) properties of a word* <u>*sustains*</u> *memory for the word,* <u>*whereas*</u> *attention toward the structural properties of a word leads to memory that* <u>*declines*</u> *more rapidly.*

3. *In the* <u>*academic*</u> *world there is no* <u>*substitute*</u> *for being* <u>*aware*</u> *of recent research findings on memory and learning and* <u>*adjusting*</u> *instructional practices* <u>*logically*</u> *based on these findings instead of ignoring or blindly* <u>*rejecting*</u> *new developments.*

4. *Our mental* <u>*networks*</u> *sometimes remain relatively* <u>*stable*</u> *but at other times* <u>*expand*</u> *rapidly, increasing our* <u>*capacity*</u> *to perform different tasks, such as understanding and speaking English or any other* <u>*target*</u> *language.*

Step 6. Put the four statements (which contain all 20 target words) on a screen at the front of the class to allow students to double-check their understanding of the sentences. Tell them that they can change their answers if they would like to do so.

Step 7. Ask students to compare their answers with one or two other students in the class. Then tell the class that all four statements were intended to be true. If there is any disagreement, discuss and clarify further the meaning of each statement.

Step 8. Ask students to share any other ideas they have about research on memory and learning in the field of psychology and in the academy at large. Ask them if they know of any other variables, in addition to generating items on one's own, that facilitate memory and learning. As they arise, use opportunities to include target words in the discussion.

Step 9. Tell students that one of their assignments to complete before the next class is to find out something new to contribute to the discussion on variables that affect memory and learning. Challenge them to find a variable that has not been mentioned so far. Also ask them to study and review the 20 target words in preparation for a vocabulary quiz at the beginning of the following class.

Step 10. At the beginning of the next class, administer a vocabulary quiz that asks students to write 15 of the 20 target words when provided with definitions and/or examples and to write definitions for the other 5 target words.

Step 11. Ask each student to write on the board his or her new piece of information on research on memory and learning and lead a discussion about the new information, incorporating variants of the word families of the 20 target words as opportunities arise.

Commentary

In addition to implementing key principles of the IBI approach in a general way, Step 1 in this lesson gives students an important opportunity to hear each target word form before providing definitions for words in Step 2. In turn, Step 2 demonstrates that one straightforward method of providing meaning-bearing comprehensible input is to define words. This method is meaning bearing because words are inherently meaningful, and it is comprehensible because the meaning of words is being explained, at least when the vocabulary used in the definitions provided is accessible to students at their current level of proficiency. As suggested by IBI Principle 10, this lesson also applies a research finding that is directly applicable to vocabulary instruction: the positive effects of opportunities to generate target words on one's own. Step 4 applies this research finding in an affectively positive manner, allowing students to attempt to retrieve target words on their own outside of the context of a quiz or test before being given a quiz later on in Step 10.

LESSON 2

Our Future in the Face of Hurricanes

Target Words: *adjacent, albeit, collapse, compile, conceive, convince, enormous, forthcoming, integrity, invoke, likewise, nonetheless, notwithstanding, odd, persist, pose, reluctance, straightforward, undergo, whereby*

(Words taken from AWL Sublist 10; Coxhead, 2000)

Step 1. Provide students with the passage "Causes and Impacts of Hurricanes." Ask them to read the text for meaning and also to try to learn the bolded words while doing so.

Reading Passage for Step 1

Causes and Impacts of Hurricanes

As explained on www.weatherquestions.com, hurricanes are the result of areas of intense low pressure over warm ocean waters. The fuel source of hurricanes is water vapor that is evaporated from the surface of these waters. When the vapor condenses, it forms clouds and rain and warms the surrounding air. If this release of heat **persists** (continues), heat can build up and create a low-pressure center with **adjacent** (next to) winds spiraling inward around the center, the center being the eye of the hurricane. As this process continues, hurricanes **undergo** (experience) gradual change and over time can become **enormous** (huge). It is often difficult to **conceive** of (imagine) how big they can become until actually seeing them on a map. These types of hurricanes **pose** (present) serious danger, **albeit** (although) usually only after they hit land. Strong winds and massive rain can test the **integrity** (sound, unimpaired condition) of buildings and cause them to **collapse** (fall down).

Notwithstanding (in spite of this), weather scientists have ways of **compiling** (collecting) data **whereby** (by which) they can inform us about **forthcoming** (about to happen) hurricanes. Their warnings are often **straightforward** (direct, easily understood), calling for evacuations in certain areas. In such cases, local governments often **invoke** (call on) their authority to make evacuation orders. **Likewise** (in a similar way), they make statements in the media to **convince** (persuade) locals who may show **reluctance** (hesitation) to obey these orders to do so. **Nonetheless** (in spite of this), as **odd** (strange) as it may seem, some locals do not evacuate.

Step 2. Ask for a student volunteer to read the passage out loud to the entire class, and have students raise their hands if they have questions about any of the vocabulary in the text. Other students in the class and the instructor can provide information about the meanings of the vocabulary in the text as inquiries arise.

Step 3. At the front of the class, display a screen that lists all 20 target words on the left side and their corresponding synonyms or brief definitions from the text on the right side. Say each target word, and have the class work together to match each target word with its synonym or brief definition. After each match, mention key alternative meanings of the target words that would be difficult to infer from the text. For example: *To <u>conceive</u> can mean to imagine but it can also mean to become pregnant. <u>Odd</u> can mean <u>strange</u>, but in its plural form it can refer to the <u>odds</u> of a bet. For example, at a horse race, one horse may have 3-to-1 <u>odds</u>, whereas another has 99-to-1 <u>odds</u>.*

Step 4. Tell students that they will be reading the text again and that this time they should attempt to fill in empty blanks with the missing vocabulary (the following version of the text can be used for this purpose). Let them know that *notwithstanding* and *nonetheless* are largely interchangeable but that they should use each of these terms only once. After students have had enough time to attempt to fill in the blanks alone, have them work with one or two partners to double-check their answers. Display a version of the text with the correct answers on a screen at the front of the class.

Step 5. Tell students that they are now going to discuss the best ways for people to improve their abilities to deal with hurricanes in the future and how to work to prevent or diminish the effects of hurricanes (if possible). Ask students to share their ideas.

Step 6. Have students view a video (or read a short article if you prefer) about Bill Gates's efforts to obtain patents on using barges to cool surface waters in order to decrease the strength of hurricanes (a search using "Bill Gates hurricanes" on YouTube should provide options). Ask students the following questions (which include target words):

1. Do you think the plan is odd, or do you find it convincing?

2. Could enormous Category 5 hurricanes undergo some sort of change using this method?

3. Can you conceive of any other ways to prevent or reduce the impact of hurricanes?

Step 7. Put the list of the 20 target words (without their definitions) on a screen at the front of the class. Ask students to try to remember which of the words has more than one meaning and to explain those different meanings.

Step 8. As an out-of-class activity, ask students to write a half-page essay about their thoughts on the in-class discussion, particularly with regard to our future

Reading Passage for Step 4

Causes and Impacts of Hurricanes

As explained on www.weatherquestions.com, hurricanes are the result of areas of intense low pressure over warm ocean waters. The fuel source of hurricanes is water vapor that is evaporated from the surface of these waters. When the vapor condenses, it forms clouds and rain and warms the surrounding air. If this release of heat _____ (continues), heat can build up and create a low-pressure center with _____ (next to) spiraling inward around the center, or the eye of the hurricane. As this process continues, hurricanes undergo (experience) gradual change and over time can become _____ (huge). It is often difficult to _____ of (imagine) how big they can become until actually seeing them on a map. These types of hurricanes _____ (present) serious danger, _____ (although) usually only after they hit land. Strong winds and massive rain can test the _____ (sound, unimpaired condition) of buildings and cause them to _____ (fall down).

_____ (in spite of this), weather scientists have ways of _____ (collecting) data _____ (by which) they can inform us about _____ (about to happen) hurricanes. Their warnings are often _____ (direct, easily understood), calling for evacuations in certain areas. In such cases, local governments often _____ (call on) their authority to make evacuation orders. _____ (in a similar way), they make statements in the media in order to _____ (persuade) locals who may show _____ (hesitation) to obey these orders to do so. _____ (in spite of this), as _____ (strange) as it may seem, some locals do not evacuate.

in the face of hurricanes. In the essay they should use at least 10 of the 20 target words from this lesson. Also have them prepare to take a short quiz on all 20 of the target words in the next class.

Step 9. In the next class, collect the essays and then administer a vocabulary quiz in which students are given full definitions for 10 of the target words and asked to write the 10 corresponding words. For the rest of the quiz, select 5 of the target words that have more than one meaning and ask students to write the multiple meanings. (If there are two meanings, provide spaces for two meanings; if there are three, provide spaces for three meanings.)

Commentary

The positive effect of providing opportunities to generate target words (per Principle 10) is once again incorporated in this lesson. This time it is incorporated in

Step 3 in the context of a reading passage that contains all of the target vocabulary for the lesson—of course *after* students have had opportunities to process the target words as input in Steps 1 and 2. Principle 5 is incorporated in that the target words that appear in the passage in Step 2 are bolded, thus enhancing them compared to the rest of the vocabulary in the passage. Principles 7–9 are also clearly incorporated in this lesson when one considers the gradual buildup from processing words as input in the initial steps, to considering multiple word meanings in Step 7 (but not in the earlier steps), to writing an essay that includes some of the target words in Step 8. This sequencing clearly demonstrates respect for different stages of development of vocabulary knowledge and a progression from less demanding to more demanding activities over time (Principle 9).

Notice also how target words can be incorporated seamlessly within a larger discussion focused on a meaningful topic. The questions for class discussion presented in Step 6 demonstrate how this can be done: *Do you think the plan is odd, or do you find it convincing? Could enormous Category 5 hurricanes undergo some sort of change using this method? Can you conceive of any other ways to prevent or reduce the impact of hurricanes?* Here, five target words have been recycled as input while focusing students' attention on meaning-related issues pertinent to the topic of the lesson. Students may or may not notice that the target words have reappeared, but either way, they once again will be exposed to these words as input within a larger communicative context that focuses on the topic of the lesson.

LESSON 3

What Is Your Method of Cleaning a House or Apartment?

Target Words: *apron, blend, bulb, collapse, compliment, concrete, devise, drip, fragrant, gross, insert, lease, ledge, mess, pail, skip, tile, tub, unique, vacant*

(Words taken from 5,000-word level of the Vocabulary Levels Test)

Step 1. Ask students to view a brief video (no more than 2 minutes) related to a very messy house (a search using "messiest house" on YouTube provides a number of examples; the Style Network show *Clean House* may provide some other ideas), and then ask them questions about the video using as much of the target vocabulary as you can. Tell students to ask for the meanings of any words they do not understand. When they do, provide the meanings for them. For example: *Was the house shown in the video vacant or did it have occupants? Did anything in the house look like it was going to collapse? . . . Collapse means to cave in and fall down. How dirty was the tub they showed in the video? Did you think what you saw was kind of gross? . . . Gross means disgusting. Do you think this house was unique in terms of how dirty it was as compared to other houses you've seen?*

Step 2. Tell students that in preparation for a discussion on house cleaning you will be showing pictures related to 20 target words that will facilitate the discussion. Use a previously prepared picture file to present all of the target words (even the verbs and adjectives with less transparent meanings can be depicted; clarifications about meanings can be made when presenting the words). Show each picture and describe it, focusing on the target word in question and repeating it during the presentation. For example: *This is an apron. People generally use aprons when they are cooking as opposed to cleaning but they can be used along with plastic gloves when cleaning to keep cleaning products off of your clothes. This is a light bulb. Bulbous plants like carrots or turnips are also bulbs, but when talking about cleaning we'll generally be talking about light bulbs. This picture depicts the verb to blend. See how the person in the picture is combining two different colors of paint? The result will be a blend. The person in the picture is blending the two colors of paint.*

Step 3. Tell students that you will be doing a quick review of the target words. Go through each picture and say its corresponding word, but do so much more quickly this time.

Step 4. Display all 20 words on a screen at the front of the class and ask students to give as many examples as they can think of showing how the words relate to cleaning a house or apartment.

Step 5. Ask students about the last time that they spent a substantial amount of time cleaning a house or apartment. Ask them if they have any particular method of doing so: In what room do they start? Why? Where do they finish? Why? And so on.

Step 6. Do a total physical response (TPR) activity using a number of the lesson's target words. The TPR activity should demonstrate a particular set of cleaning tips. For example: *To really clean the floor of the tub in your bathroom, which is looking pretty gross at the moment, you'll need a small pail (or bucket) and some cleaning products. Hold up the pail and pour in the cleaning products. Blend a couple of different types together in the pail. But make sure they don't produce an unexpected chemical reaction. The sides of the tub look pretty clean, so just skip those for the moment and focus on the ledge of the tub and the area near the drain. Also, you'll see that the faucet in the tub is dripping, so you'll have to get that fixed at some point.*

Step 7. Have students complete this activity outside of class: Go to the following Style Network webpage and pick one of the videos on cleaning tips to summarize for other students in the next class: www.mystyle.com/mystyle/shows /cleanhouse/videos/index.jsp. When summarizing the cleaning tip that you chose, make sure to include at least two to three of the target words for this lesson.

Step 8. In the next class, have students summarize the cleaning tip video that they viewed for the class.

Step 9. Display all of the pictures of the 20 target words at the front of the class, and ask students to try to recall them on their own by writing them on a sheet of paper. Students should work alone first and then in pairs as needed to generate the appropriate target words.

Step 10. Go through the list of target words again and ask students if they know of any secondary meanings of the words. Fill in missing information about alternative meanings as you go through the list with the entire class. For example: *Your house can be a <u>mess</u>, and your finances can also be in a <u>mess</u>. Does that make sense? You can change a light <u>bulb</u> in your house, and some plants, such as tulips, also grow from <u>bulbs</u>. <u>Concrete</u> is a material that you find on some floors, but ideas or words can also be <u>concrete</u> as opposed to abstract.* Answer any questions that students might have as you progress.

Commentary

Principle 10 (application of research findings) is incorporated in this lesson by presenting the target words in Step 3 at a faster rate than in Step 2 (rate variability positively affects L2 vocabulary learning). Note also that TPR (as in Step 6) can be an enjoyable and effective manner of presenting target words as input even for learners at more advanced levels. Additionally, note that target words become, in a sense, recycled as input when the instructor focuses on multiple L2-specific meanings, as demonstrated in Step 8 and which is consistent with IBI Principle 8.

LESSON 4

Getting a Home Loan or Refinancing After the Housing Crisis

Target Words: *amortization, appraisal, bailout, cash flow, contract, depreciation, downturn, equity, expenses, income statement, interest rate, kudos, liabilities, line of credit, margin, recession, revenue, risk, stimulus, tenacity*

> (Words taken from the list of Financial/Banking and Accounting Terminology on http://businessvocabulary.org)

Step 1. Tell students that in the next class you want to discuss some issues related to getting a home loan or refinancing after the most recent housing crisis but that you need them to learn some key vocabulary first. Provide them with a sheet of paper that lists all 20 of the target words ("words" also being used to refer to phrases and expressions here) on one side and definitions on the other. Also instruct the students to do the following activity outside of class using the website http://businessvocabulary.org: For each of the 20 words, read the definition of the word on the website and then view the video containing the spoken form of each word and its definition. Do this for all 20 words, and repeat the process as many times as needed until you think you know the words fairly well. At that point, go to the side of the sheet where definitions-only are written and write as many of the target words as you can alongside their corresponding definitions.

Step 2. When students arrive in the next class, ask them to try to recall, without looking at their lists, the words that you asked them to study. Let them say as many as they can remember on their own, and then say the remaining target words if students do not generate all of them on their own.

Step 3. Tell students a story or provide an analysis related to the lesson topic. The story or analysis should contain all of the target words. You can give students a written copy of the story or analysis if desired. For example: *I know someone who recently tried to refinance his condominium in order to get a lower <u>interest rate</u>, but he ran into a lot of difficulties. All he wanted was to know what his <u>expenses</u> would be, the <u>amortization</u> of the refinanced loan, the <u>margin</u> between his expenses and gains in doing the refinancing, and any other pertinent details of the <u>contract</u>, but things were more complicated than he expected. They asked him to do several <u>appraisals</u> of the value of his condo to see if the condo had appreciated or suffered <u>depreciation</u> in value, to determine the exact value of <u>equity</u> he had in the condo, to provide a formalized <u>income statement</u>, and to list all of his current <u>liabilities</u>. Evidently, the economic <u>downturn</u> in the economy made the refinancing process more challenging, and the bank <u>bailout</u> and the <u>stimulus</u> program put into place by the federal government did not make things much easier for him even though he had more than sufficient yearly <u>revenue</u> so as to pose little <u>risk</u> to the lender. Because his <u>cash flow</u> was not great, he had to take out two loans, one of which was a <u>line of credit</u>, in order to complete the refinancing, but ultimately he got the refinancing done. I say <u>kudos</u> to him for his <u>tenacity</u> in being able to get the refinancing during such a bad <u>recession</u>.*

Step 4. Ask students what they think this story (or analysis) indicates about getting a home loan or refinancing after the most recent economic crisis. Also ask what suggestions they would give to someone interested in getting a loan or refinancing in this type of economic climate.

Step 5. Have students work in groups of two or three to prepare a list of formal suggestions to assist someone who wants to get a loan or refinance today. Have each group include at least five of the target words from this lesson as well as two or three new vocabulary words that they find to be appropriate to complete this list. Have each group first define the new vocabulary that they used and then present their list of suggestions to the rest of the class. Have a discussion about the extent to which the lists of suggestions do or do not overlap.

Step 6. Give students a list of definitions (and/or examples) of the 20 target words, and ask them to try to recall and write the appropriate word for each definition (and/or example). After students have made their best efforts, go over the answers with the entire class.

Step 7. Working in the same groups of two or three, students should attempt to write as many suggestions as they can think of (if any) to improve the process of refinancing. This time their suggestions should be for lending institutions as opposed to individuals interested in getting a loan or refinancing.

Commentary

Step 5 in this lesson demonstrates how IBI activities can lead to vocabulary learning that goes beyond any specific list of target words. Steps 4 and 5 demonstrate how learners can become actively involved with the topic at hand fairly quickly after having at least some exposure to target words as input (in Steps 1 and 3, with Step 2 providing opportunities for target word retrieval). The critical point here is that the target words be presented as meaning-bearing comprehensible input before students are asked to produce or elaborate on the words (Principles 6 and 7). The lesson also demonstrates how IBI activities can be pertinent and informative to conditions of the modern world. Both businesspeople and individuals in other fields could benefit not only from learning the target words in this lesson but also from considering the various suggestions that students generate for individuals and lending institutions.

LESSON 5

What Is the Best Way to Be Healthy and Stay in Shape?

Target Words: *ache, aerobics, blood pressure, calorie, crouch, dehydration, fracture, harmful, jog, joint, obesity, potent, pulley, regimen, resistance, rush, savvy, smorgasbord, squat, wince*

(Words taken from the Health, Fitness, and Nutrition
list at www.vocabulary.com/lists/25156)

Step 1. Using a previously prepared picture file for all of the target words, show each picture to the class, say the target word to which it refers, and make any clarifications needed as to why the picture refers to the word in question. Substantial teacher–student interaction can be included. For example: *Blood pressure. This picture shows a person taking her blood pressure. It looks like it is 120 over 80. Is that a healthy range? Calorie. You can see the arrow in this picture pointing to the number of calories in the product. Crouch. The person in this picture is crouching. See how his back is bent forward so much toward the top. That is crouching. Dehydration. This is when your body needs more water. See how the athlete looks dehydrated in the photo? She is drinking to replenish fluids.*

Step 2. Using electronic versions of the same pictures used in Step 1, have students view three additional repetitions of each target word using a computer presentation program. Present the words in two groups of 10, showing the first 10 three times and then the second 10 three times. For each word, have the picture appear first, followed by the written form of the word below the picture 6 seconds later, followed by the spoken form of the word 2 seconds after that, and then allow the picture and the written form of the word to remain on the screen 2 additional seconds. Instruct students to try to remember each target word on their own (without saying them out loud) and then to confirm their answers (again, in their mind only) when they see and hear the written and spoken forms of the words.

Step 3. Tell students they are going to answer some questions related to health and exercise in order to start a conversation about the best ways to be healthy and stay in shape. Hand out a sheet with the following questions. Have each student write their own answers to the questions. Then go over the questions as a class, and determine any trends that emerge in the answers. Discuss what the answers indicate about the class's ideas about the best ways to be healthy and stay in shape.

1. *Do you count <u>calories</u> every day?*

2. *What are your food and exercise <u>regimens</u> like?*

3. *How often do you check your <u>blood pressure</u>?*

4. *Have you ever stopped rushing in your life in an effort to lower your <u>blood pressure</u>?*

5. *When <u>jogging</u>, doing <u>squats</u>, or working with <u>pulleys</u> on exercise machines, do your joints ever <u>ache</u>?*

6. *When exercising, have you ever done something that was <u>harmful</u>, such as <u>fracture</u> a bone or cause your back to <u>ache</u> for an extended period of time?*

7. *When doing <u>aerobics</u>, have you ever become overly <u>dehydrated</u>?*

8. *When doing <u>resistance</u> training, have you ever <u>winced</u> because you felt so much pain?*

9. *Do you pay attention to your posture and avoid <u>crouching</u>?*

10. *Do you think high rates of <u>obesity</u> are tied to how often people eat at buffets or <u>smorgasbords</u>?*

11. *Do you consider yourself a <u>savvy</u> individual when it comes to diet and exercise?*

12. *In your opinion, what is the most <u>potent</u> method of staying healthy and in shape?*

Step 4. Have students work in the same pairs as in Step 3. Each pair should generate a list of five suggestions for staying healthy and in shape using the target words of this lesson as appropriate. Have each pair share their suggestions with the rest of the class. Discuss the extent to which the suggestions did or did not overlap and why.

Step 5. As an assignment for outside of class, ask students to do the following: (1) At www.vocabulary.com/lists/25156 click on each of the 20 target words for this lesson in the Health, Fitness, and Nutrition list. For each word, click on the button to listen to the word and then read all of its definitions and usage examples. For at least three of the target words, write down meanings that were not used in class today and a usage example for each of these alternative meanings and bring them to class. (2) Explore other words in the Health, Fitness, and Nutrition list. Select at least one other word that you believe other students may not know, and bring it to class along with a definition in your own words and an example of the word in an original sentence. (3) Go to the www.vocabulary.com main page and answer at least 10 of the vocabulary questions in The Challenge section. Make a mental note of how well you did, and if you answer incorrectly for some words, remember at least one of those words and bring it to class. Feel free to do more than 10 words if you like in order to continue to try to improve your vocabulary.

Step 6. Ask each student in the class to share her or his response for Number 1 in Step 5. Continue until students have exhausted all of the alternative meanings that they noted.

Step 7. Ask each student to share his or her response for Number 2 in Step 5. Write each new word on the board when spoken by the student. Make sure the definitions and examples of these new words are correct and help all students in the class understand them.

Step 8. Ask each student how she or he did with Number 3 from Step 5. Ask the class if they thought the activities were fun and useful. Ask them if they will continue using www.vocabulary.com independently to continue to improve their vocabulary. Ask them what other online sources they are using (if any) to improve their English vocabulary. On the board, list sites that students find to be helpful. Select some additional sites that you would like to share with students, such as www.lextutor.ca (by Tom Cobb) and www.lognostics.co.uk (by Paul Meara) or other appropriate online resources that were described in Chapter 1. If possible, pull up these websites on a screen at the front of the class to show students how they work.

Step 9. Ask students if anyone has changed their mind about the series of suggestions that they wrote in the last class about good health and staying in shape.

Step 10. As an assignment for outside of class, have each student select and read a current article related to being healthy and staying in shape and write a half-page summary and reaction paper about the article. Have students select three new words from their article to share with the class (in the next class period). Also tell students that there will be a quiz on the 20 target words for this lesson at the beginning of the next class.

Step 11. At the beginning of the next class, administer a 20-item vocabulary quiz. Each item is a sentence with a missing blank for one of the target words. At the front of the class, display the 20 pictures used for the target words in Steps 1 and 2. Each sentence on the quiz should exemplify the meaning of the word in question while making reference to the picture. For example:

1. *This picture shows a person taking her _____. It is 120 over 80.*

2. *This picture shows the number of _____ in the product. These are units of energy.*

3. *This picture shows a man who is _____. His upper back is bent forward.*

Step 12. Have students summarize and give their thoughts on the health-related article that they read for the assignment in Step 10. To facilitate understanding, first make a vocabulary list on the board by having students write the words that they selected and their definitions. Each student's article summary should lead to additional class discussion of the topic.

Commentary

Steps 5–8 and 10–12 demonstrate how the IBI approach can be used to promote the type of vocabulary acquisition that goes beyond a given set of target words for a particular lesson. Step 2 puts Principle 10 in place by presenting words using multiple talkers and by providing opportunities to generate target words, both of which positively affect L2 vocabulary learning. Step 8 helps to provide students with tools to improve their own independent study of English vocabulary. These facets of Lesson 5 stand out along with its overall input-first orientation and, as with the other lessons in this chapter, its incremental progression in the steps.

CHAPTER 5

Lessons for Your Classroom, Part II: Reading as a Primary Source of Input

Whereas Chapter 4 exemplified input-based incremental (IBI) vocabulary instruction using a variety of sources of spoken and written input in a distributed manner, this chapter focuses on how to apply the IBI approach when using reading as a primary source of input. We begin with some basic background information about effective second language (L2) reading instruction, including the psycholinguistic processes involved in reading and an approach to instruction that views reading as a process and consists of prereading, guided reading, and postreading activities. This discussion is followed by five IBI lessons based on a variety of different types of readings, including a website about a major tourist destination in Australia, a position paper by a well-known feminist journalist and political activist, a prologue to a play by perhaps the most renowned writer in the English language, a book chapter (also made into a movie) by a prolific contemporary U.S. novelist, and a one-page reading on the origins of agriculture from the reading section of a TOEFL practice test. These readings were selected to demonstrate how the IBI approach can be used to promote vocabulary learning while working with any type of reading, regardless of length or content. As was the case in Chapter 4, the lessons make use of online resources and are designed so that instructors of English as a second or foreign language (ESL/EFL) can select among them and implement them on different occasions in their classrooms.

The lessons and commentary presented in this chapter also are consistent with the views on vocabulary and reading and the eight techniques for promoting L2 vocabulary learning proposed by Barcroft (2004b):

1. Use textual enhancement to enhance target words in the text.

2. Increase the number of times target words appear in the text.

3. Use glossing to clarify the meaning of target words.

4. Present target words as input during prereading activities.

5. Include activities on target words during prereading activities.

6. Instruct learners to attempt to learn target words in the text.

7. Encourage learners to use dictionaries as needed.

8. Include activities on target words during postreading activities.

Of course, a number of considerations come into play when deciding whether to modify texts or create texts according to Techniques 2 and 3, and it certainly may not be desirable to do so on most occasions. But for some types of readings, such as readings created by the instructor, it can be valuable to make use of these techniques for text modification.

EFFECTIVE READING INSTRUCTION: PREREADING, READING, AND POSTREADING ACTIVITIES

Reading involves both bottom-up and top-down processing. Bottom-up processing involves reading the letters and words of the text to extract meaning, whereas top-down processing involves relating one's prior knowledge (schema) of the topic of a text to fill in information as needed. In order to help learners comprehend texts better, Lee and VanPatten (1995) suggest (1) preparing learners and helping them activate appropriate schemata, (2) providing guided interaction as learners work through a text, (3) promoting assimilation of information when working with a text, and (4) personalizing and exploring the communicative functions of a text. Suggestion 1 can be accomplished by means of a variety of prereading activities, such as brainstorming; focusing on titles, headings, and illustrations; using world knowledge; using pretests and posttests; and scanning for specific information in a text. Suggestion 2 can be accomplished through guided interaction activities while learners are reading. Suggestions 3 and 4 can be accomplished with various types of postreading activities.

A focus on promoting knowledge of new vocabulary within a text can accompany these larger goals of increasing comprehension in a seamless manner. Presenting target vocabulary at the prereading stage not only helps to activate background knowledge on a topic; it also helps to fill in information that may be lacking with regard to the topic of a given reading. Similarly, focus on vocabulary during postreading activities only contributes further to consolidating one's understanding, assimilation, and personalization of a text. The more new vocabulary in a text is understood, the better on all of these fronts. The IBI lessons that follow demonstrate this argument more clearly.

PROMOTING BOTH INCIDENTAL AND INTENTIONAL VOCABULARY LEARNING DURING READING

The application of IBI Principle 3, which is to promote both incidental and intentional vocabulary learning, can have a substantial impact on increasing the amount of new vocabulary that students learn during reading. As mentioned previously, a number of studies have demonstrated that vocabulary learning during reading is greater when participants are instructed explicitly to learn target words in a text (Barcroft, 2009; Hulstijn, 1992; see also Paribakht & Wesche, 1997). However, if a text is sufficiently comprehensible, learners also have opportunities to pick new words incidentally (without intending to do so), and these opportunities need to be appreciated as well. These features of the IBI approach to teaching vocabulary during reading should be apparent in the five sample lessons in this chapter.

DIRECTLY APPLICABLE RESEARCH FINDINGS ON READING AND VOCABULARY LEARNING

With regard to IBI Principle 10, which suggests applying directly applicable research findings, it should be noted that some research findings are directly applicable to L2 vocabulary learning during reading and others are not. For example, the benefit of providing explicit instructions to learn new words during reading (Barcroft, 2009; Hulstijn, 1992) is directly applicable to L2 reading, as are the benefits of increasing the number of times target words appear in a text (Hulstijn, Hollander, & Greidanus, 1996; Rott, 1999), allowing learners to use bilingual dictionaries during reading (Hulstijn et al., 1996; Luppescu & Day, 1993), providing marginal glosses in written texts (Hulstijn et al., 1996), and using multiple hypertext glosses in computerized texts (Yun, 2010). However, the benefit of increasing talker or voice-type variability when presenting target words in spoken input (Barcroft & Sommers, 2005) would only be applicable during activities that accompany text-focused activities. This point should be kept in mind when considering which research findings to apply.

DEGREES OF EXTENSIVE INDEPENDENT (OR FREE) READING

What makes reading, including extensive reading, truly *independent* or *free*? One answer is that this type of reading should be purely, or at least largely, for one's own enjoyment. Another answer is that this type of reading happens only when one has sufficient knowledge of the vocabulary in a text so as not to have to constantly look up words in a dictionary or become frustrated often trying to infer meanings of words and phrases from context when there is not sufficient context to do so (or both). These two views—we will call them the "independence-enjoyment" and the "sufficient vocabulary knowledge" viewpoints—both have important implications when it comes to truly independent or free reading. The following paragraphs consider these two viewpoints as related to ideas proposed by researchers (and instructors) about extensive free reading and L2 vocabulary learning and the tenets of IBI vocabulary instruction.

The Independence-Enjoyment Viewpoint

As mentioned previously, Krashen (1989, 1993) argues in favor of extensive free voluntary reading as a means of helping learners improve their L2 vocabulary knowledge, an argument that is consistent with the independence-enjoyment viewpoint. The IBI approach has no qualms at all with this approach in the sense that extensive independent reading (or extensive independent listening) affords numerous benefits, with regard not only to vocabulary learning but also to other aspects of L2 acquisition. The IBI approach also takes no issue with the idea that reading (or listening) often should be voluntary. When specific readings are to be assigned, instructors should attempt to select—and novelists, poets, philosophers, and others should strive to write—texts that are enjoyable, engaging, informative, and so forth. There are really only two main concerns with this approach from the IBI perspective: (1) Will enough vocabulary be learned incidentally using this approach? (2) Will lack of knowledge of vocabulary in the text ultimately impede truly independent and enjoyable reading?

Krashen (1989) argues for the value of free reading for L2 vocabulary learning by emphasizing how learners in the studies reviewed were indeed *able to* acquire words during free reading. A critical limitation of this approach, however, is that many of the studies cited in the review did not compare incidental vocabulary learning during reading with other methods available for vocabulary instruction, such as more direct methods. Without comparing the effects of free reading on vocabulary learning to Option B, Option C, or some other option, it is difficult to make claims about the relative effectiveness of free reading.

As mentioned previously, early studies on incidental pick-up rates for vocabulary learning during reading were fairly discouraging. To provide one example, Nagy, Anderson, and Herman (1987) calculated that the probability of learning a new word from context is between 5% and 20%. The 5% figure was used to calculate that, upon reading a million words in 1 year, children can learn 1,000 words per year (Nagy et al., 1987; see also Nagy, 1997; Nation & Waring, 1997). However, this figure does not indicate the number of words that could have been learned in the same amount of time using alternative methods of vocabulary instruction. Other research has examined factors that affect one's ability to guess word meanings from context (Liu & Nation, 1985), the impact of different strategies for inferring word meanings (e.g., Paribakht & Wesche, 1999), and the positive effects of variables such as topic familiarity and L2 reading proficiency

(Pulido, 2003) on L2 incidental vocabulary learning. Additionally, more recent studies have demonstrated more encouraging pick-up rates than earlier studies. For example, Horst (2005) used an innovative methodology to assess word gain and found higher growth rates than did earlier studies, and Pigada and Schmitt (2006) demonstrated substantial vocabulary gains (pick-up rate of about 1 of every 1.5 words tested during a month) albeit based on a case study only. Schmitt (2010) notes some of the earlier, more discouraging findings may have been related to methodological problems.

Nevertheless, when incidental versus intentional orientations during L2 reading are directly compared, intentional orientation readily wins out (e.g., Barcroft, 2009; Hulstijn, 1992)—on the order of 3.50 words versus 4.51 (a gain of approximately 29%) overall in Barcroft's (2009) study—as do reading plus direct-instruction activities as compared to reading only (Paribakht & Wesche, 1997). The results of these studies, in which learners increased vocabulary when they were only instructed to try to learn new words and told that they would be tested on them or were instructed directly on vocabulary in addition to reading, speak volumes when compared to studies that strive to maintain incidentally oriented orientations (see also Prince's [1996] demonstration of the superiority of translation-based learning over the provision of sentence-level context only, which bodes against relying heavily on context). As one final example, in a recent study, Yamamoto (2011) compared L2 incidental vocabulary for reading (control) versus extended reading (read for at least 30 minutes every day outside of class and five books during a 13-week semester) groups. Yamamoto's results indicate that, "contrary to expectations, no significant increase was shown in the amount of productive vocabulary size" (p. 226) between the two groups. Imagine, however, what gains might have been made if intentional vocabulary learning had been involved instead of extended reading only.

Given the limited pick-up rates demonstrated by research on incidental L2 vocabulary learning, instructors need to consider what they may be losing in terms of vocabulary gain when relying exclusively or extensively on free voluntary reading alone. Even if only 30% of student activity in a course involves free voluntary reading, one needs to consider how much more vocabulary might have been learned if additional interventions are included, such as asking learners to attempt to learn new words in the text (promoting an intentional orientation), engaging learners in different types of complementary direct-instruction techniques, or both. Note also that these techniques are very different from direct or explicit grammar instruction when students are asked to consider issues about the target language. Direct vocabulary instruction promotes acquisition of the target language because vocabulary is the place where form meets meaning and where form–meaning connections are made at a very basic level (cf. Ellis, 1994). For example: *Here is a picture of a <u>dandelion</u>. The word is pronounced "<u>dandelion</u>," and what it refers to is that yellow flower you see in the picture. Some people consider it a* *weed*. A *weed* is a plant that you probably don't want growing in your garden or in your yard. Do you have a lot of *dandelions* in the region where you live?* This is input-based language learning, not explicit learning *about* language as in the case of explicit grammar instruction.

In light of these considerations and the many desirable aspects of having learners engage in voluntary free reading, instructors have some important choices to make. The approach to vocabulary instruction proposed in this book is more than friendly to the idea that reading (or listening) should often be independent and, as often as possible, enjoyable. It also proposes being realistic about what we can reasonably expect in terms of vocabulary gain when we rely on independent free reading (or listening) alone. For this reason, Principle 3 advocates promoting both intentional and incidental vocabulary learning in a thoughtful manner.

The Sufficient Vocabulary Knowledge Viewpoint

The second concern about free extended reading (or listening) alone is whether lack of knowledge of vocabulary in a text will impede truly independent and enjoyable reading. Anyone who has read a text for which he or she lacked knowledge of much of the vocabulary can relate to this concern. It can be quite frustrating and unenjoyable. Ideally, we might like for an extended reading to be at a sufficiently comprehensible $i + 1$ level (Principle 4), but this is not always easy to achieve (even when working with graded readers, and readings of this nature go against the idea of truly free and voluntary reading because students are not allowed to select from all available texts in which they might be interested).

If an instructor identifies which vocabulary in a text is likely to be unknown (Principle 1) and uses a series of IBI lessons to teach this vocabulary in pre-reading activities, moving from different chapters or segments of the text (or listening) in a piece-by-piece manner, students are afforded with opportunities to read the text and *understand* the target vocabulary while reading. This can be a delightful experience, especially when compared to the alternative of having to look up words frequently, attempting to infer word meanings from context when sufficient context is often not available, or both. Webb (2008) demonstrated that learners pick up more word meanings when sentences contain more contextual clues, confirming that sufficiently rich context does matter. But to provide such context on a regular basis in extended readings would imply altering sections where context is insufficiently rich, in other words, altering the novel, play, or other type of reading itself, something that seems largely unacceptable. Marginal glosses with definitions in hypertext versions of readings may be a better solution because these do not alter the reading itself per se.

A drawback to this approach is that we are no longer dealing with a situation of truly independent reading, but in following the approach, students could still be allowed to select their own text and work independently on identifying novel vocabulary in the text, particularly if they are working with an electronic version of the text and can use electronic resources such as those available at Tom Cobb's Lexical Tutor (www.lextutor.ca). Computer-based IBI activities can then be designed for those students, and they can complete them independently. In fact, if students are to select among a limited number of extended readings (e.g., a selection of 20 novels), pre-prepared computer-based IBI lessons could be available for each segment of the reading (e.g., each chapter of a given novel) for each student to complete independently on the computer while gradually making her or his way through the novel. This approach supports the students' independent work while helping to ensure that they have sufficient vocabulary knowledge to be able to enjoy the process of reading the novel.

IBI APPLICATIONS TO EXTENSIVE FREE AND NOT-SO-FREE READING (OR LISTENING)

Whatever the degree to which an instructor chooses to equip students with knowledge of target vocabulary in a reading (or listening) prior to reading (or listening), the IBI approach is available to help, ensuring that the manner in which the novel vocabulary is presented will be meaning oriented, even if it is presented prior to reading (or listening) and not encountered in a more incidentally oriented context. As mentioned earlier, the only potential drawback of the approach concerns the degree of independence of the reader (or listener). Even if the IBI lessons in question are completed outside of the classroom using computer-based materials, this is still not the same as "select any book that you like and read it for enjoyment." In making decisions about the extent to which IBI vocabulary instruction will be used in this context, instructors might want to put themselves in learners' shoes and then carefully decide which option they would prefer: (a) less than completely independent reading but better knowledge of the new vocabulary in a reading beforehand or (b) more independent reading but with less knowledge of the new vocabulary in the text.

Additionally, instructors can make the decision about how much vocabulary to teach beforehand and how much independence to allow in extensive reading (or listening) in degrees and not as an absolute either/or manner. The more target words are taught beforehand, the less independent the reading, at least in principle. Similarly, the less teaching of target words beforehand, the more independent the reading (or listening), at least in principle. But as we have seen, lack of knowledge of words in a text (or listening) leads to lack of independence (needing to look up words frequently or try to infer meaning that is often insufficiently transparent) and, potentially, lack of enjoyment. Each instructor, after considering the issues from the standpoint of the student, can make informed decisions in this regard.

Additionally, instructors can apply research findings (Principle 10) that are applicable to incidental L2 vocabulary learning regardless of whether full IBI lessons are to be included during extensive reading. For example, if a text does not have marginal glosses for novel words, an instructor might create a version of the text that includes them or might ask students to learn (intentionally) any novel words in the text (per research findings indicated in Table 2.2 in Chapter 2). Pedagogical interventions of these sorts might be viewed as less "independence-robbing" than others.

Two extensive readings were selected for two of the sample lessons presented in this chapter: a play by Shakespeare and a novel by Stephen King. Target words are identified and taught in prereading, guided reading, and postreading activities for segments of these extensive readings. Additional IBI activities would need to be created and implemented for all of the other segments of these works (i.e., chapters of the novel or acts of the play). These two sample IBI lessons involve activities to be carried out both inside and outside of the classroom, but if an instructor (or course developer or instructional material developer) desires to do so, these two lessons could be modified so that any students could complete them outside of the classroom on their own and thereby be able to read the play or the novel and complete the IBI activities in a more independent manner. The commentary following these two lessons includes suggestions on how they could be adapted in order to be completed outside of the classroom in this more independent fashion.

TEXT SELECTION AND COMPREHENSIBILITY

When selecting texts, it is important to consider how difficult it will be for students to understand them and how many opportunities they will offer for students to improve their vocabulary knowledge and other aspects of their linguistic competence. IBI Principle 4 maintains that meaning-bearing comprehensible input, particularly Krashen's proposals regarding $i + 1$, should be used when presenting target words as input. Although the construct may be difficult to operationalize when working with real-world constraints, if an instructor (or language program director, etc.) can select a text at the $i + 1$ level, that text should provide solid opportunities for learners to pick up new vocabulary, not only when they are explicitly taught the new vocabulary in the text as part of the larger set of reading-related activities but also when they are presented with opportunities to acquire new words incidentally without explicit instruction of the vocabulary in question. The five texts selected for the lessons in this chapter are targeted toward high-intermediate-level ESL/EFL learners, some leaning more toward the intermediate and others more toward the advanced level.

LESSON 1

About the Great Barrier Reef
(www.greatbarrierreef.org/about.php)

Target Words: *barrier, clam, coral, ease of access, first hand, heritage, marine, mollusk, parallel, reef, reptile, sponge, to breed, to seek after, to stretch, vessel, vivid*

Step 1. Inform students that they will be learning and engaging in a discussion about the Great Barrier Reef, in Australia. Present all of the target words (word forms only) on a screen at the front of the class. Assign each student one or two words from the list of target words to present to all of the other students on the next day of class. Instruct students that they should provide clear definitions of examples of their terms and that the use of visuals is encouraged. Also instruct them that they should expose the other students to at least five repetitions of the word forms so that they have a better chance of learning them.

Step 2. At the beginning of the next class, have all students complete their presentations. Assist them when help is needed regarding the pronunciation or meaning(s) of the target vocabulary.

Step 3. Ask students if they have ever visited a large reef before and, if so, what they saw and whether they liked the experience and, if so, why. Then ask them if they have visited the Great Barrier Reef. Lead a discussion that stimulates students' background knowledge regarding reefs and, in particular, the Great Barrier Reef.

Step 4. Open the page www.greatbarrierreef.org/about.php on a screen at the front of the class, and ask students what they think of the pictures. Scroll down to go through the main headings of the online reading, and ask students if the sections are clear to them.

Step 5. As another activity to be completed outside of class, ask students to read the online page on the Great Barrier Reef at home and to make a list of points from the reading that they feel are important. Also instruct them to explore other webpages related to the Great Barrier Reef and to write at least one other interesting point not mentioned in the assigned online reading. Finally, let students know that there will be a quiz on the target words for this lesson and that they should study for the quiz before the next class.

Step 6. In the next class, administer a short quiz on the target words of this lesson. For half of the words, provide the word and ask students to write definitions. For the other half, provide definitions and ask students to produce the target word forms.

Step 7. Pull up the online reading again. Ask students to summarize the main points they found in each section (noting each subheading). After going through the main points of the reading, ask all of the students to share the additional points they found out about the Great Barrier Reef from their explorations online.

Step 8. As an activity to promote assimilation and personalization of the information, ask students to work in pairs to develop a list of the top three reasons for visiting the Great Barrier Reef and the top three activities that they would like to do there. In both lists, students should incorporate as many of the target words as possible.

Commentary

Steps 1 and 2 of this lesson provide a good example of how IBI Principle 2 can be accomplished outside of a primarily teacher-led activity; this lesson is quite student centered from the beginning. Step 3 is an activity that can help to activate learners' background knowledge on the topic, whereas Step 8 provides an opportunity for learners to assimilate and personalize information. Certainly, the lesson could be expanded to include more steps, such as steps that focus on other L2-specific meanings and usage of the target words (Principle 8), but all of the basics of the IBI approach are employed while relying on an online reading (albeit a fairly short one) as a primary source of input.

LESSON 2

"A Balance Between Nature and Nurture,"
by Gloria Steinem
(www.npr.org/templates/story/story.php?storyId=4805246)

Target Words: *activist, core, dignity, either-or, engraving, enlightening, feminist, heredity, hierarchy, house trailer, inauthentic, nurture, preordained, primordial, suffragette, to align, to awaken, to craft, to feature, tombstone, ton of bricks*

Step 1. Write and circle the word *feminism* on the board, and ask students to brainstorm ideas and events they associate with this word. As they provide responses, create different branches in a semantic map as a means of activating students' background knowledge related to feminism. If nobody mentions Gloria Steinem, ask students if they know who she is. Continue to facilitate a conversation about Gloria Steinem, filling in historical background information as appropriate. Then ask "What does it mean to be a feminist?" and continue the discussion of the topic.

Step 2. Let students know that they will be reading a short essay written by Gloria Steinem titled "A Balance Between Nature and Nurture." Ask them what they think the article might be about based on the title only.

Step 3. Display the subset of the target words (including phrases) in the essay itself (not from the NPR introduction) on a screen at the front of the class. Tell students that all of these words appear in the article. Go through all of these words and define them for the students, using examples as needed. Then ask students what they think the article might be about now that they know some of the words that appear in it.

Step 4. Provide each student with a sheet of paper that contains all of the target words, with those that appear in the NPR introduction asterisked. Tell students that the words with asterisks appear either before or after the actual essay in what they are going to read.

Step 5. Have students work in pairs to read different segments of the essay. After each segment, have students write the main idea(s) of the segment (working together). Show each segment on a screen at the front of the class by using the text available on the NPR website.

Step 6. After all segments are completed, ask students to summarize the reading. What were the key points?

Step 7. Give students a list of definitions (on a separate sheet of paper) of the target words in the text, and ask them to try to recall them. Go through the definitions with the class, and make sure every student has the correct word for each definition.

Step 8. Tell students that they will be reading the essay again while also listening to Gloria Steinem read the essay herself. Tell students that they will be asked to summarize the main points of the essay and to indicate the extent to which they think there is evidence to support Steinem's assertions. Show the entire essay and play the audio portion on the NPR website, allowing students to read and listen to the essay.

Step 9. As an assignment to be completed outside of class, ask students to make a list of the key assertions presented in the article. After each point, students should indicate on a scale of 1 to 10 how much evidence (1 = no evidence; 10 = abundant evidence) they believe there is to support each assertion. Also tell students that there will be a quiz on the target vocabulary from the essay at the beginning of the next class. Let them know that the quiz will provide definitions only so that they will have the opportunity to attempt to write the correct term for each definition.

Step 10. At the beginning of the next class, collect the assignment and administer the vocabulary quiz.

Step 11. Ask students what they believe to be the key assertions of the essay, and lead a class discussion regarding the students' thoughts on the assertions.

Commentary

In addition to the activation of schemata in prereading activities (Steps 1–3) and assimilation and personalization of information (Steps 9–10), focus on the target vocabulary is never lost throughout the lesson; it is maintained as part of the focus on the content at hand (IBI Checklist Items 2 and 3 in Figure 3.1). The fact that students are allowed to read the text more than once is consistent with Principle 2, and the use of both written and spoken versions of the essay can be viewed as a form of input enhancement (Principle 5). The rest of the lesson is consistent with the other principles of IBI, focusing on presentation of the target words as input first and then gradually increasing difficulty and output (with access to meaning) over time.

LESSON 3

"Romeo and Juliet"
(Act 1, Prologue), by William Shakespeare

Target Words: *foes, grudge, mutiny, loins, overthrows, piteous, rage, strife, to strive, to mend, toil*

Step 1. Request any appropriate permissions to use an online version of the text, and, if permissible, add hypertext glosses for the target words in question. An online version can be found at http://shakespeare.mit.edu/romeo_juliet/full.html.

Step 2. Have students take a few minutes to think about the people they consider to be the greatest writers in their native language. Have each student write the names of the writers that he or she considers the three greatest writers. Going language by language, have students give their opinions about the greatest and, in each case, state why.

Step 3. After all of the students' native languages have been covered, ask students to take another few minutes to write down the names of three writers that they consider to be the greatest writers in the English language. Get feedback from each student. If William Shakespeare is mentioned, ask students what they know about him and which works by Shakespeare they are familiar with. (If Shakespeare is not mentioned, ask students the same questions anyway.)

Step 4. Present the students with the list of target words from the reading and their corresponding definitions. Go through the words and the definitions.

Step 5. Tell students that they will be reading a segment of a famous play by William Shakespeare, and ask them to guess which play it is, based on the target words that they have seen. The guesses and discussion should lead to "Romeo and Juliet." Ask students if they know where the play takes place. Ask if any of the students have visited Verona and, if so, what it is like. Show some pictures of Verona on a screen at the front of the class. Ask what the students think Verona was like at the time that "Romeo and Juliet" was written. Also ask them about family feuds and grudges and how these might have played out at the time that the play was written.

Step 6. Tell students that before reading the segment of "Romeo and Juliet" you will be talking a bit more about the target words and how they are used in the modern world. Go through each word and talk about how it is used. For example: *A _grudge_ is something that people hold against each other when one person does something wrong to someone else. Can you think of any children of famous people who have held _grudges_ against their parents? Here are some examples. . . . _Mutiny_ is when a group of people revolt and take over some authority, such as taking over a ship by deposing the captain. Can you think of any modern examples of _mutinies_? Here are some examples. . . .*

Step 7. Give students a matchup activity in which they need to map target words with their definitions, and go over it as a class.

Step 8. Assign "Romeo and Juliet," Act I, Prologue, as a reading to complete outside of class. Tell students that they will have a brief practice quiz on both the content of the Prologue and the target words at the beginning of the next class and (if hypertext glossing was possible) that they can click on any of the target words to retrieve their definitions.

Step 9. At the beginning of the next class, administer a quiz in which definitions are provided and students are asked to produce the target words, along with a few questions about the main content of the Prologue.

Step 10. Have students work in pairs with a copy of the Prologue in front of them. Ask them to go through it together line by line and do their best to understand each line.

Step 11. Go through the segment together with the entire class, asking students to clarify any lines that they do not understand.

Step 12. Ask students to work in groups of three to see if they can think of any modern-day counterparts to the situation and events described in the Prologue. Go over their ideas as a class.

Step 13. Present students with a list of target words from the Prologue in order of the frequency with which they appear in modern-day English (using an online source or otherwise). Ask them to reflect on why some of the target words are used so much less frequently than others in modern-day English.

Commentary

Step 1 incorporates Principle 10 by taking advantage of the benefits of providing hypertext glosses during reading (Yun, 2010). In addition to schema-activating prereading activities (Steps 2 and 3) and an assimilation/personalization-focused postreading activity (Step 10), Steps 4 and 6 follow Principles 2 and 4 (repetition of target words in contexts of meaning-bearing comprehensible input). Providing opportunities to retrieve target words using output with access to meaning is also apparent in Steps 7 and 9. Step 8 is consistent with Principle 3 in that learners are instructed not only to read the text for meaning but to make attempts to learn target words in the text intentionally, which research indicates to be more effective than relying on incidental L2 vocabulary during reading alone. The lesson also demonstrates how a potentially very challenging text can be handled if approached in an input-based, meaning-focused, and incremental manner.

Optional Modifications for Students to Be Able to Do the Lesson Independently

If an instructor (or course developer or instructional material developer) wishes to create a version of this lesson that can be completed independently outside of the classroom, consider the following possible adjustments that can be made to the lesson. Change Steps 2 and 3 so that they are done online individually (having students generate a list of the top three writers for their native language as well as for English). For Step 4, have students view a prepared audiovisual presentation of the words online instead of providing the input directly in the classroom. Steps 5 and 6 also should be presented in an audiovisual format on the computer. For Step 5, students can simply answer questions individually, and predetermined feedback can be provided. The electronic presentation for Step 6 can be either an audiovisual presentation with an instructor presenting the terms or just audio with pictures that correspond to each target word as it is discussed using the audio file. Steps 7–9 require minimal modification except to convert instructions and the activities themselves into a computer-based format and to provide appropriate time frames for when to complete the activities that don't correspond to "the next class." Have students do Step 10 individually. For Step 11, have students access a recording of someone reading the Prologue so that they can hear it and read it at the same time. Some additional auditory commentary on the segment could be included, but this is optional. Create a version of Step 12 that allows students to do it individually and write their responses on the computer. Provide a computer-based presentation of the frequency ordering for Step 13 and have students provide responses individually on the computer.

LESSON 4

Rita Hayworth and Shawshank Redemption
(Chapter 2), by Stephen King

Target Words: *aspirations, Attorney General, bungalow, clever, con, frame-up, infidelity, jury, revenge, scandal, spectacles, to cheat, to clip, to convict, to limp, to mitigate, to muffle, to smuggle, to sneak around, trial*

Step 1. Give students a list of the titles of all of Stephen King's novels. Have them mark with checkmarks all of the books that they have read or movie adaptations that they have seen. Once they have finished, go through the list and ask students to raise their hands for each work they have read or movie version of which they have seen.

Step 2. Ask students how they would describe the work of Stephen King, such as with regard to the themes and character types he tends to focus on.

Step 3. Tell students that you will be showing them a series of pictures associated with the target words (and phrases) for the chapter of a novel by Stephen King that the class is going to read. Show the pictures and discuss the meaning of each target word. For example: *To smuggle refers to when someone enters a place with some type of product that is prohibited. In this picture, you can see the suitcase of someone who tried to smuggle a bunch of cell phones into a different country and got caught. The smuggler got caught. Clever is an adjective used to describe someone who is creative and smart. In this picture, you can see a comic strip in which a cow connects a radio directly to an electric fence to get power. It is a clever idea, and the cow is clever to think of it. Spectacles is another word for glasses. Spectacles is kind of an old-fashioned word, though. Most people say* glasses *instead of* spectacles *in everyday usage these days. In this picture I might call these glasses spectacles* [showing a picture of someone wearing an old-fashioned style of glasses, i.e., "spectacles"] *but would be less likely to call these glasses spectacles* [showing a picture of someone wearing a much more modern style of glasses]. *The two terms can sometimes be used interchangeably, but I think "glasses" is by far the more commonly used term today.*

Step 4. Ask students if they can guess the Stephen King novel in which these target words appear. If nobody guesses correctly, tell students that it is from *Rita Hayworth and Shawshank Redemption*. Ask them what they know about the theme of the novel. Talk about the location in which it takes place and some basic introductory information about the plot, which could be done in the form of a summary of what takes place in Chapter 1.

Step 5. If possible, provide learners with a version of the chapter that includes marginal glosses for the target words, and allow them to use dictionaries during reading.

Step 6. Have students read the first line of every paragraph of the chapter and try to write one sentence summarizing what they think will occur in the chapter. After writing their sentences, students can share their ideas with the rest of the class.

Step 7. Have students return to the text and read not only the first sentence of each paragraph but the entire text. Have them underline any target word that they encounter while reading. Ask them to try to use context to infer meaning if they cannot remember the meaning of any of these words. Also have them circle any other vocabulary that they did not previously know and try to infer the meaning of those words as well.

Step 8. Ask students what they think about the chapter and whether they would be interested in reading the rest of the book. Why or why not? Discuss the plot of the chapter together. Ask students what they think the major themes of the book are going to be.

Step 9. Go over any other words that students circled and explain the meaning of those words. Write this new target vocabulary on the board, and ask students to add them to the list of target vocabulary related to this chapter. Tell students that there will be a practice quiz on all of the target vocabulary (including the vocabulary on the board) on the next day of class and that it will be tied to the chapter.

Step 10. At the beginning of the next class, provide students with a copy of the same chapter but with blank numbered spaces where the target words had appeared. Ask them to try to fill in the numbered spaces with the correct target words. After they finish, go over the sentences with the target words and check the students' answers.

Step 11. Ask students to prepare (individually or in pairs) a series of questions that the narrator of the chapter might be interested in asking the character Andy (who is described in the chapter).

Commentary

Step 3 of this lesson provides a good example of how IBI Principle 2 (present target words as input frequently and repeatedly) can be incorporated in a pre-reading activity that serves to activate learners' background knowledge related to a text. Steps 1–4 are all prereading activities that help to activate learners' background knowledge. Step 5 incorporates Principle 10 by attempting to take advantage of the benefits of marginal glosses and dictionary use (Hulstijn, Hollander, & Greidanus, 1996). Step 9 takes advantage of opportunities to focus on words to be turned into target vocabulary, which is consistent with IBI Principle 3. Step 10 also helps students benefit from the positive effects of opportunities for target word retrieval.

Optional Modifications for Students to Be Able to Do the Lesson Independently

Create an individual version of Steps 1 and 2 to be completed either online or on a worksheet that students are given before they begin reading the novel. For Step 3, create an online audiovisual file that presents the target vocabulary as input in a similar manner. Of course, there cannot be the same back-and-forth interaction as in the classroom, but one option would be to create a video of the target vocabulary presentation in a classroom and allow students, working independently, to view it. Create a question-and-answer version of Step 4 that students can complete on a worksheet or the computer. Step 5 requires no change. Modify Steps 6 and 7 so that students can complete them individually. Have students do Step 8 individually online and prepare a sheet with answers and information so that they only have to click to retrieve them. For Step 9, have students type in (on the computer) any words that they did not know. Pre-prepared written definitions, explanations, and examples of any words a student types should appear when the student types in the words. Modify Step 10 so that it can be done individually, changing the part in which answers are gone over in class to an online version that provides the appropriate answers after students have attempted to provide them. Step 11 needs very little modification except that students should complete it on a worksheet or on the computer while working independently.

LESSON 5

"Neolithic Agriculture Development"
(Practice Test 1, pp. 453–459), from
Cambridge Preparation for the TOEFL Test (4th ed.)

Target Words: *corollary, cultivate, ditch, domestication, evaporation, hierarchical, independently, irrigation, mill, Neolithic, salinity, sediment, settlements, sickles, surpluses, to breed, to gather, to migrate, to reap, trade*

Step 1. Tell the class that they will be reading a one-page text on the origins and development of agriculture in human societies but that you want to focus on a set of target vocabulary within the text first. Divide the class into groups, assign specific target words to each group (e.g., three to four words per group), and let each group know the paragraphs in which these words appear. The task of each group is to present each target word and its definition to the class. The groups should attempt to infer the meaning of the words they are assigned from the context of the paragraphs in question, and when presenting each word, they should repeat the word form at least three times.

Step 2. After the groups have attempted to infer the meanings of the target words, provide a list of definitions (without the target words to which they correspond) to help the groups determine if what they inferred corresponds to a definition in the list.

Step 3. Have each group present their target words to the rest of the class. If there are errors, help by correcting them and making reference to the correct definition on the definitions sheet. Ask students not to write any of the target words being presented until after all are presented. Ask them only to try to remember the target words at this stage.

Step 4. After all target words have been presented, ask students to attempt to write all of the target words next to their corresponding definitions on the sheets.

Step 5. Go over the definitions, and ask students who did not present the words in question to attempt to remember them. If they cannot remember a word, help out by saying the correct word and its definition (repeating the word form again).

Step 6. Ask students how much they know about the development of agriculture in human societies, and lead a brief discussion on the topic based on their responses.

Step 7. Have students quickly skim the passage, focusing on the first sentence of each paragraph. When they finish, ask them to write a sentence indicating what the major focus of the passage will be.

Step 8. Ask students to read the entire passage and to try to confirm the extent to which what they wrote in their sentence was correct or not. After they have finished writing, they should write another sentence indicating the extent to which the first sentence was correct or not.

Step 9. As a class, discuss students' responses to Steps 7 and 8.

Step 10. Have students quickly review the list of target words and their definitions on a screen in front of the class.

Step 11. Ask students to complete the additional questions following the text. Many of these concern the target vocabulary and other vocabulary in the text.

Step 12. Go over the answers to these questions as a class.

Step 13. Ask students to make a list of as many challenges as possible that human beings faced during the development of agriculture and to identify which of these we still face today.

Step 14. Go over students' responses in a discussion with the entire class.

Step 15. In the next class, show a series of pictures that represent the target vocabulary (either directly or indirectly). Ask students to try to write the words that correspond to each picture (giving hints and clarification as needed, particularly for any picture that does not obviously depict a target word).

Step 16. Go over the answers with the class.

Commentary

This lesson demonstrates how the IBI approach can be used to promote learning vocabulary in readings in TOEFL practice tests well beyond what would otherwise be the case if students were to complete the readings and questions in the book only. The qualitative difference in learning outcomes when using the IBI approach should be clear. Steps 1–3 focus on identifying target word meanings from context but with support so that these words can be presented as input for other students in a student-centered manner. Steps 4 and 15 provide important opportunities for students to attempt to retrieve target words on their own. All of the other steps are consistent with an approach to reading as a process, one in which learners are encouraged to activate preexisting knowledge related to the topic in prereading activities, to assimilate information in the text in postreading activities, and to interact with the text in ways that facilitate comprehension in guided interaction during reading. The focus on target vocabulary prior to reading should facilitate comprehension of the text, and the focus on target vocabulary in postreading activities should help to ensure that this vocabulary becomes even further consolidated in memory. Additionally, the application of the IBI approach to TOEFL practice readings such as this one should be much more engaging to learners as compared to doing the activities in the book alone.

CHAPTER 6

Designing Activities to Supplement Your Existing Materials

Whereas the previous two chapters focused on the application of input-based incremental (IBI) vocabulary instruction as an independent approach in contexts that involve a variety of sources of input (Chapter 4) or reading as a primary source of input (Chapter 5), this chapter focuses on how the approach can be used to supplement other existing instructional materials. The IBI lessons presented in this chapter were designed to supplement target vocabulary that appears in three English as a second or foreign language (ESL/EFL) instructional texts with very different instructional foci: (a) a grammar book that includes noun/adjective/verb + preposition constructions and phrasal verbs that can be treated as target vocabulary, (b) a multipurpose textbook that includes target vocabulary in each chapter, and (c) a book that focuses on vocabulary based on pictures.

WHEN SHOULD I SUPPLEMENT?

When can IBI vocabulary instruction be used to supplement your existing course materials? A short answer to this question is: anytime when new vocabulary is (a) not presented in the input with sufficient repetition, (b) not presented using meaning-bearing and sufficiently comprehensible input, and (c) not treated in a manner that respects the incremental nature of vocabulary learning. From this perspective, an even shorter answer to the question is: very often! Textbooks focused on grammar, functional use of the language, or specific purposes (e.g., business, medicine) often lack sufficient repetition of target words in the input and sufficient treatment of vocabulary in an incremental manner. Even textbooks designed to focus on second language (L2) vocabulary learning, such as "reader" texts designed to promote L2 vocabulary learning during reading, suffer from similar limitations.

It is beyond the goals of this book to analyze the relative effectiveness of the immense quantity of instructional texts available today. Instead, our goal is to equip instructors—and program directors, curriculum developers, publishers of instructional materials, and so forth—with the tools needed to apply the IBI approach in a wide array of contexts, including when it is useful to do so in a supplementary capacity while working with existing instructional materials.

SUPPLEMENTING A WIDE RANGE OF INSTRUCTIONAL MATERIALS

As mentioned earlier, the IBI lessons presented in this chapter were designed to supplement target vocabulary that appears in three ESL/EFL instructional texts with very different instructional foci: *Grammar in Use: Intermediate* (Murphy, 2009), *New Headway: Upper-Intermediate Student's Book* (Soars & Soars, 2005), and the *Oxford Picture Dictionary* (Adelson-Goldstein & Shapiro, 2009). Numerous other types of instructional texts could have been selected, but these three were selected because of their popularity and because they focus on distinct aspects of linguistic development, providing an opportunity to demonstrate the wide range of areas in which IBI vocabulary instruction can be adapted.

LESSON 1

What Are Your Thoughts on Computer Tablets?

Target Words: *attitude toward, damage to, delighted with, demand for, disappointed by, impressed with, to apologize to, to cheer up, to collide with, to concentrate on, to consist of, to doze off, to figure out, to look forward to, to mix up, to plug in, to search for, to specialize in, to stare at, to wave back*

(All of these noun/adjective/verb + preposition combinations and phrasal verbs appear in Murphy's [2009] *Grammar in Use: Intermediate*. The selection is a small subset of the combinations and phrasal verbs presented on pp. 252–284.)

Step 1. Tell a story related to computer tablets in which you can include, define, and exemplify the target vocabulary for this lesson. Use at least some pictures from a picture file as visual support when telling the story and clarifying the meaning of the target phrasal combinations. For example: *Do you think demand for computer tablets like the iPad and the Blackberry Playbook is increasing? Demand for a product increases when more people want to buy it, as in how much supply there is of a product and the demand for it. A friend of mine who specializes in computer science recommended that I buy a computer tablet, but my attitude toward it is a bit mixed. I already have a laptop, and in general I'm delighted with it. It's great, at least when I have a place to plug it in. When I'm at home I just plug in the cable to the outlet on the wall and never run out of battery. (Here is a picture that shows how easy it is to plug in a laptop when you're near an outlet at home.) But when I travel, it sometimes is really difficult to find a place to plug it in. What are your attitudes toward the different computer tablets? Are you impressed with them or disappointed by them? Here is a picture of someone who is delighted with her computer tablet. I think she may specialize in computers like my friend does. Does it look to you like she specializes in computer science? At any rate, she is clearly delighted* *with the computer tablet and has a very positive <u>attitude toward</u> the features it offers. Why is she so <u>impressed with</u> it? I guess I'm pretty <u>impressed with</u> some of the features they have too. Besides not having to <u>plug</u> them <u>in</u> as often, you can . . . .*

Step 2. Provide students with a sheet of paper. On one side should be a series of pre-prepared activities similar to those used in *Grammar in Use: Intermediate* for the target vocabulary; on the other side should be a list of the target vocabulary. The activities should include cloze and sentence-completion activities such as those used in the book, but all of the sentences should be opinion statements related to the topic of the lesson (computer tablets). For example: *One reason not to buy a computer tablet is that you can* _____ *the computer tablet cables with the cables from your laptop* [answer: *mix up*]. Ask students to attempt to fill in the blanks or complete sentences using the target vocabulary. When they aren't sure of the target word, they can turn over the sheet to see the options.

Step 3. Go over the correct answers on the sheet. Have students take turns giving the correct answer by reading each sentence out loud. Once the correct response is given, students should indicate whether or not they agree with the content of the statement.

Step 4. Make a list of different types/brands of computer tablets currently available. Have students form groups, and assign a specific type/brand of computer tablet to each group. Tell them that their task is to find out more information about the tablet in question and to present the information to the rest of the class on the next day of class. Also let the class know that there will be a quiz on the target vocabulary at the beginning of the next class.

Step 5. At the beginning of the next class, give a vocabulary quiz in which the students need to complete sentences or fill in blanks with correct target words based on the context of the sentences (the contexts should be very clear).

Step 6. Allow the different groups to meet to discuss what they learned about their assigned computer tablet. Give each group some time to prepare a summary of information about the tablet in question for the rest of the class. Have all groups do their presentations.

Commentary

This lesson demonstrates how an IBI lesson can be used to go well beyond the presentation of noun/adjective/verb + preposition combinations and phrasal verbs as lists with definitions. This lesson gives examples on presenting this vocabulary in a truly meaning-oriented context with multiple repetitions of the vocabulary in the input in order to help learners acquire it. Whereas the treatment of the vocabulary in the textbook (*Grammar in Use: Intermediate*) is limited to lists of vocabulary with definitions and examples followed by cloze and sentence-completion activities, the IBI activities in Lesson 1 above should help bring the target vocabulary to life by providing a truly meaning-oriented communicative context in which to work with every target item. The lesson is consistent with other IBI principles as well, including Principle 10 in that it provides students with multiple opportunities for target word retrieval (Steps 2 and 5) after the target words have been presented as input (and repeatedly so, as in Step 1). This provision can be incorporated frequently in IBI lessons, as evidenced by lessons in previous chapters, given the substantial research vying for its effectiveness (as indicated in Table 2.2 in Chapter 2).

LESSON 2

Walking Around in Wonderful Cities

Target Words: *aroma, boutiques, brand-new, cosmopolitan, down-and-out, dull, lively, magnet, mouthwatering, packed, pedestrianized, shabby, to buzz, to dash around, to flock, to snore, trendy*

> (All of these words, with some minor modifications, appear in Soars and Soars's [2005] *New Headway: Upper-Intermediate Student's Book*, p. 119.)

Step 1. Distribute to all students pre-prepared pictures from a picture file. On the back of each picture should appear a target word and a clear explanation of what the word means and how it relates to the picture in question. Ask students to view their pictures and to study the definitions and explanations on the back of the pictures so that they can show the pictures to the rest of the class and explain the meaning of the words in question. Ask them to repeat each word at least four times when talking about the picture and explaining the meaning of the word.

Step 2. Have all students give their presentations of the target words and their meanings using the picture files. Assist and provide linguistic support when appropriate.

Step 3. Have students complete all of the activities (Numbers 1–7) related to the Soho district in London on p. 119 of the book prior to the next class.

Step 4. In the next class, go over Numbers 1–7, including some examples of the mini-essays that students wrote for Number 7. Collect the work done outside of class.

Step 5. Ask students if they have ever visited Barcelona. Whether they have or not, provide them with 17 questions about the city. Each question includes a target word. The students should answer each question based on their experience visiting Barcelona or on their own intuitions. For example: *Is Barcelona a lively city? Are the people in Barcelona always dashing around, or are they laid back? Are there any shabby areas of town? What is the most trendy area of Barcelona, and why?*

Step 6. Go over the answers with students, making sure they understand the meaning of the target words while leading a discussion on what the city of Barcelona is like. If possible, display online resources and pictures on a screen at the front of the class to facilitate the discussion.

Step 7. Ask students to draw comparisons between London and Barcelona based on the reading in their book and the discussion that they just had (including information and photos from the Internet). What are the similarities and differences between the two cities?

Commentary

This lesson provides a good example of how Principle 2 does not imply teacher-led activities in order for target words to be presented frequently and repeatedly in the input. It also demonstrates how IBI activities can be used to supplement an existing lesson in a fairly seamless manner; instead of focusing only on Soho and London as content, the content now becomes both London and Barcelona. Note how Step 3 asks students to complete all of the original activities in the *New Headway: Upper-Intermediate Student's Book* version of the lesson while providing additional support (particularly additional repetition of the target vocabulary in the input in this case) in all of the other steps. The IBI-supplemented version of this lesson not only includes additional provisions to promote effective learning of the target vocabulary, it also expands the focus of the content of the lesson, which in turn may lead to additional benefits in terms of both linguistic competence and general knowledge.

LESSON 3

Fixing Up a Fixer Upper

Target Words: *backhoe, bricks, bulldozer, ~~cherry picker~~, concrete, construction worker, crane, drywall, ~~I beam/girder~~, insulation, ~~jackhammer/pneumatic drill~~, ladder, ~~pickax~~, plywood, ~~scaffolding~~, shingles, shovel, sledgehammer, stucco, tile, to hammer, to install tile, to lay bricks, to paint, trowel, window pane, wood/lumber—cul de sac, magnolia tree, squirrel, stock market, swan*

> (All of the words before the dash appear in Adelson-Goldstein and Shapiro's [2009] *Oxford Picture Dictionary*, p. 178. In an effort to avoid the potential negative effects of presenting target words in semantic as opposed to thematic sets, the five crossed-out terms were replaced by the terms in bold that appear after the dash.)

Step 1. Prepare an audiovisual presentation for all of the 22 (finally selected) target vocabulary items on p. 178 and the 5 new items that replaced others in an effort to break up the semantic set. The presentation should include different pictures of the terms from p. 178 along with pictures that depict the other 5 terms. Use a different talker or a different speaking rate for each of the six repetitions of each word. The talkers or speaking rates should be interspersed completely at random or as randomly as possible. Make this audio presentation available online for students.

Step 2. Tell students that in the next class you will be focusing on how to repair things on a house and perform small- or large-scale construction projects. Ask them to study the target vocabulary by listening to the pre-prepared audiovisual presentation. Also tell them that there will be an ungraded practice quiz on the words on p. 178 in the next class.

Step 3. In the next class, administer a matching practice quiz using target items and their corresponding pictures. These can be different from those on p. 178 provided that each picture clearly represents the word to which it corresponds.

Step 4. Go over the answers with the class. When going over the terms, say them out loud and mention alternative meanings and uses as opportunities arise. For example: *Yes, that is a crane, but a crane is also a bird with a very long neck, and crane can also be used as a verb, such as when a person cranes her neck to try to see something. . . . Right, that material is called concrete. Concrete can also be used as an adjective, such as when someone provides a concrete example, meaning a precise and tangible example. The use of concrete as an adjective in this way makes sense if you think about how concrete as a substance is very solid and stable. You can't miss it! . . . Correct, that refers to the stock market. Actually, it is a picture of the stock market on Wall Street. Those are buyers and sellers. Do they look happy? I can't think of any alternative meanings for the term stock market in and of itself. . . . That is insulation as a material that insulates a building. There are also more metaphorical uses of the word. For example, you might say that a child has led a very insulated life, meaning that he has been protected, maybe overprotected, from the outside world. Is there anyone who you think has led an insulated life?*

Step 5. Show the class a large picture of a house in a dilapidated state. Ask the class what kind of reconstruction projects the house needs. As different types of projects are mentioned, ask students to describe how the construction would be done. The construction projects should lead to usage of the target vocabulary on p. 178. If students struggle with other nontarget vocabulary (not on p. 178), help to fill in with the missing vocabulary and write the new vocabulary on the board. For example: *Right, the house definitely needs a new roof, and the broken part there is the gutter. A new gutter probably needs to be installed, too.* [Write the word *gutter* on the board.] *Do you think that magnolia tree on the right damaged the gutter? How do you know it is a magnolia tree? Look at the flowers . . . .*

Step 6. Ask students if any of the target vocabulary reminds them of a time when they worked on a construction project on a house or another type of structure. Listen to one or two responses and then divide the class into groups of three to four students. Ask the groups to discuss the biggest repair or construction project they can remember doing. Group members should describe to each other, in as much detail as possible, what they did to complete the project. Then, as a group, they should come to a conclusion about which student in the group completed the biggest repair or construction project and why.

Step 7. Have each group share their conclusions with the rest of the class.

Step 8. As an assignment to be completed outside of class, ask students to write a short essay (half-page to one page) on how to complete a construction or remodeling project that involves a substantial amount of vocabulary from p. 178.

Step 9. At the beginning of the next class, collect the essays.

Commentary

The *Oxford Picture Dictionary* can be a useful resource for helping students develop their vocabulary knowledge, particularly when it comes to the wide array of concrete nouns that need to be learned in the L2. However, it tends to present target words in semantic sets, which has been found to have negative effects on L2 vocabulary learning due to interference (Finkbeiner & Nicol, 2003; Tinkham, 1997). This lesson demonstrates how some potential target words in a semantic set can be replaced by others to decrease the extent to which the target words pertain to one semantic set only and the extent to which the previous grouping may cause interference (as demonstrated in the removal and replacement of at least some of the target words for this lesson). The lesson also demonstrates how target words can be presented in the input to students outside of a teacher-led activity. Steps 1–3 apply Principle 10 by taking advantage of transferable research findings, namely, that L2 vocabulary is improved when the teacher (a) presents target words with talker or speaking-rate variability and (b) provides learners with opportunities to retrieve target words (as indicated in Table 2.2). Step 4 applies Principle 8 by focusing on a wider range of L2-specific meanings and uses of the target vocabulary. Step 5 is consistent with Principle 3 in that the activity looks to promote learning of nontarget vocabulary, however incidentally or intentionally, by putting on the board vocabulary that is new to at least some students in the class. The lesson is meaning focused and content focused. Consistent with the philosophy of IBI vocabulary instruction, it first provides learners with opportunities to process the target words and input and then pushes them to increase their knowledge in an incremental manner. Finally, this lesson provides an example of how the number of target vocabulary items can vary from lesson to lesson. In this case, the total number of target vocabulary items was 27, going beyond the 20, the number of target vocabulary items presented in most of the other lessons in this book. Of course, the number of target vocabulary items can also be decreased well below 20 or increased beyond 27, depending upon instructional goals, time availability, the level of the students, and other contextual factors to which an instructor may be responding.

CHAPTER 7

The Future of Vocabulary Research and Instruction

The approach to vocabulary instruction presented in this book grew out of concrete research findings and a theoretical perspective that is consistent with these findings. Beyond hunches or wishful thinking, the approach stems from a series of concerted efforts to identify the implications of the results of a number of investigations combined with an application of commonsense ideas, such as with regard to Principle 1 on planning and Principle 10 on applying research findings beyond those that underlie other principles. This final chapter first clarifies and discusses foundational (and unchanging) tenets of input-based incremental (IBI) vocabulary instruction and how future research may enhance applications related to these tenets. It then discusses how the IBI approach should be enhanced by future research with directly applicable findings for second language (L2) vocabulary learning (Principle 10) and advances in technology, computer-based and otherwise. The chapter then points out areas of research that are on the rise when it comes to improving understanding of L2 vocabulary acquisition, in particular with regard to the interface between vocabulary and grammar, the distinction between quantity and quality of L2 vocabulary learning and the mental representation of words, and the neurological bases of L2 vocabulary learning and representation. We then conclude with some final thoughts on the role of vocabulary in language development and communicative competence.

FOUNDATIONAL TENETS OF THE IBI APPROACH

Some of the tenets of the IBI approach are foundational and unchanging. These include the critical roles of (1) planning for vocabulary instruction and learning; (2) providing target vocabulary as input and considering issues in lexical input processing; (3) being specific when predicting the relationship between task type, processing type, and expected learning outcomes; (4) acknowledging the incremental nature of vocabulary learning; and (5) teaching all aspects of L2 word knowledge, including L2-specific meanings and usage, over time. The following paragraphs consider each of these foundational tenets in turn and explore what instructional implications future research may have in each of these five areas.

The Role of Having a Plan

One of the tenets of the IBI approach that is unchanging is its advocating for planning when it comes to vocabulary instruction and learning. Having a plan is one of the features of the approach that is based largely on common sense, but as discussed in Chapter 2, when all of the principles were introduced and discussed, there is a substantial amount of research available to instructors, course coordinators, program directors, and developers of instructional materials regarding the process of selecting target words. One option is to consider the particular needs and goals of the student (see, e.g., Long, 2005, on L2 needs analysis). Another option is to focus on word frequency and teach the most frequent (1,000, 2,000, 3,000, etc.) words first (see, e.g., Nation, 2001). Although planning, including carefully selecting target words, is an unchanging tenet of the IBI approach, future needs analysis research related to vocabulary and future research on frequency and selection of target words may provide new information that may facilitate planning for vocabulary learning.

The Role of Input and Input Processing

Another foundational and unchanging tenet concerns the critical role of input and input processing. Providing input is critical for effective vocabulary instruction, in terms of both quantity and quality. As for quantity, the more often learners have opportunities to hear and see target vocabulary in the input, the more likely they will be able to learn it. As for quality, the target words need to appear in, and as, meaning-bearing and comprehensible input so that learners can make appropriate connections between form and meaning, which are critical in language learning across the board. Also, enhancing target words in the input (via bolding, underling, etc.) encourages learners to attend to them more readily than would otherwise be the case. Another example of improving the quality of input is to provide acoustically varied spoken input based on multiple talkers, speaking styles, or speaking rates. This type of input leads to substantially improved L2 vocabulary learning.

Present-day research and theory related to quantity and quality of input should continue to be advanced by future research on lexical input processing, providing new insights about the most effective ways to present target vocabulary in (and as) the input. One area with the potential for breaking new ground on this front is research on partial word form learning based on word fragments produced by L2 learners when they have not yet learned the complete form of a word. Barcroft (2008), for example, analyzed productions of learners after they had been exposed to 24 new L2 Spanish words using only two repetitions of each target word. The results indicate that their productions included 69% partial words versus only 31% whole words, a high percentage of one-letter fragments, and privileging for producing word-initial fragments. In another study on partial word form learning in both L2 German and Spanish, Barcroft and Rott (2010) analyzed production data after a similar vocabulary-learning paradigm and found approximately 49% more partial words than whole words, a high percentage of one-letter fragments, and, again, privileging for fragments in word-initial position in both languages.

These findings suggest that word-medial and word-final positions may be more difficult to learn. Therefore, methods of presenting target words that increase the saliency of word-medial and word-final positions—perhaps by slowing speech around these positions—might be designed to help learners attend better to letters and fragments in these positions. If research on partial word form learning continues to advance, its implications regarding learners' word-level processing patterns and effective ways of presenting target words as input should continue to grow.

The Role of Specificity in Types of Processing and Learning Outcomes

A third foundational and unchanging tenet is the need to match specific task types and the particular type of processing they invoke with different types of learning outcomes. The type of processing–resource allocation (TOPRA) model visually depicts why specificity of this nature is so critical. If someone wants to learn to play tennis, having her or him spend hours trying to balance a tennis racket on the net is task-*inappropriate*. Having her or him practice swinging the racket correctly and hitting the ball is much more task-*appropriate*. The same holds true for different aspects of vocabulary learning. If someone wants to learn a new word *form*, having him or her focus on the meaning of the target word (particularly when based on first language [L1] knowledge of the word meanings only) is task-*inappropriate*. Having him or her view or hear (or both) the target word form several times and repeatedly process it as input is much more task-*appropriate*. To make this observation implies nothing "against" focus on word meaning; it simply means that if you want to learn word form, this type of focus on meaning is not going to do the trick, at least when effectiveness is a concern, as it should be.

Whereas earlier studies on the TOPRA model focused solely on intentional vocabulary learning, more recent research has tested the predictions of the model on incidentally oriented L2 vocabulary learning during reading. Barcroft (2009), for example, demonstrates that the predictions of the TOPRA model about increased semantic processing for a semantic task (in this case, L1 synonym generation) depleting resources available for form processing (and learning) outweighed any potential benefit of the task drawing more attention to words, the end result being decreased incidental word learning during reading for a semantic task as compared to no semantic task. Additional future research on TOPRA predictions and distinctions between intentional versus incidental learning contexts should help to inform pedagogy to a greater degree in this area.

In more general terms, it is important for future studies to assess the effects of a wider range of semantic and structurally oriented tasks on both intentional and incidentally oriented L2 vocabulary learning. In addition to helping to advance theory, research of this nature will provide instructors with concrete data about what types of learning outcomes they can expect (and not expect) from an array of different types of semantic and structurally oriented tasks. Both the direction and size of the effects of these tasks should be of interest not only to the expansion of theoretical understanding in this area but also to instructors considering which tasks to use for different aims in order to provide more effective instruction.

The Role of Incremental Learning

Promoting L2 vocabulary learning in an incremental manner is another key and unchanging tenet of IBI vocabulary instruction (as confirmed by the second *I* in the acronym). During the initial stages of learning new vocabulary, learners need to be allowed to direct their limited processing resources toward processing new vocabulary as input. It is important to respect the learning burden at hand (see Nation, 2001, for additional consideration of the notion of *learning burden* in L2 vocabulary learning), which in large part involves attending to the word form that learners are hearing or reading (or viewing in signed languages or feeling in tactile languages such as Braille) and processing it as input. Later, after learners have had ample opportunity to attend to vocabulary in this manner, it is appropriate to move forward and engage them in more difficult activities that involve varying degrees of output in order to develop fluency and activities that focus on L2-specific meanings and usage of the target vocabulary.

Future research may help to fine-tune this incremental approach, particularly with regard to the presentation of vocabulary using computer-based technologies. In the classroom, more unpredictable events occur during communication, so it is difficult to follow a plan of precisely how many times a word will appear as input before a lesson moves on to the next activity. But in computer-based presentation programs in which target words appear as input, there tends to be more control in this regard. Therefore, research that involves designing and testing the effectiveness of different versions of computer-based IBI lessons should be helpful in providing more concrete recommendations in this area. Classroom-based research on the same issues certainly is possible as well, but it will need to take into account the less predictable nature of the learning setting in question.

The Role of Teaching All Aspects of Vocabulary Knowledge

Finally, teaching all aspects of vocabulary knowledge is another foundational and unchanging tenet of this approach. Just because an instructional plan is incremental in nature does not mean that one will not reach the finish line. When it comes to a given set of target L2 vocabulary, the finish line is to have knowledge of the multiple meanings and usage of the target vocabulary, including those that are L2-specific, which often involves "unlearning" L1-specific meanings and usage in order to use the vocabulary in question properly in the L2, and to develop an ability to use the vocabulary in question in a fluent manner.

Jiang (2000, 2004) is one second language acquisition researcher who has focused on the development of L2-specific meanings and usage of target vocabulary, in particular with regard to the role of L1-to-L2 semantic transfer and the gradual development of L2-appropriate semantic space for words over time. If learners have not been exposed to information about the L2-specific meanings and usage of target words, they are forced to make assumptions based on their experience with the word in L1. Jiang proposed a fairly modularly oriented model to account for what learners do when they encounter a new L2 word—a model that proposes learners start off by, in a sense, copying and pasting L1 meanings and applying them directly to the L2 words in question. After this initial transfer, they begin to develop L2-appropriate semantic space over time. Of course, more proficient L2 learners will have experienced more instances when L1 word meanings and usage do not map directly onto L2 word meanings and usage, as is so often the case. Therefore, they might be less inclined to make assumptions, but in the absence of additional (input-based) information about L2-specific meanings and usage, one is left with little choice but to make assumptions.

Following the IBI approach, it is incumbent upon the instructional program to teach L2-specific meanings and usage (Principle 8). Therefore, regardless of one's position about how modular or distributed the process should be of moving from L1-based word meanings and usage toward L2-based meanings and usage, helping learners get there is critical. Extending the work of researchers such as Jiang (2000, 2004), future studies may provide new insights with regard to the types of techniques that are most useful in helping learners make transitions to L2-appropriate meanings and usage over time. Note that Principle 7, regarding limits on forced semantic elaboration during the initial stages, is intended to apply primarily to meanings that are redundant with L1-based meanings previously acquired. If the semantic elaboration is L2-specific in nature, that type of focus should result in learning more novel aspects of meaning instead of redundant L1-based meanings.

THE IMPACT OF NEW RESEARCH FINDINGS WITH DIRECT IMPLICATIONS

IBI Principle 10 suggests making use of a wide range of concrete research findings that have directly identifiable implications for L2 instruction. Table 2.2 in Chapter 2 presented an incomplete list of research findings of this nature. These findings vary greatly in nature, but what they have in common is their immediate applicability to the development of L2 vocabulary lessons. Recall, for example, seven of these findings (see Table 2.2 for accompanying research citations):

1. Provide learners with opportunities to attempt to generate target words on their own.

2. Use thematically based (*frog, green, hop, pond, slippery, croak*) and not semantically based (*eye, nose, ear, mouth, chin*) sets of target words.

3. Increase speaking-rate variability when presenting target words in spoken input.

4. Include background music when presenting target words.

5. Allow learners to use bilingual dictionaries during reading.

6. Provide the meaning of words in marginal glosses.

7. Use multiple hypertext glosses in computerized texts.

The variety in the nature of these seven research findings is substantial, but all of them have immediately applicable implications for the design and implementation of lessons for L2 vocabulary learning.

Clearly, future research on L2 vocabulary acquisition should lead to important new research findings of this nature, and L2 instructors (and course coordinators, program directors, and developers of instructional materials) can, and should, make use of these. These new research findings are not likely to undermine other basic tenets of the IBI approach, such as the critical role of presenting target words in the input repeatedly and gradually building up different aspects of word knowledge over time. However, in light of the curiously varied range of research findings of this nature already available, the future should be very interesting in this regard. As suggested previously with regard to Principle 10, instructors may wish to keep an ongoing list of research findings of this nature in order to be able to incorporate them into lessons more easily on an ongoing basis. When it comes to effective vocabulary instruction, using this list is like opening a treasure chest, and adding new research findings to the list is like continuing to fill the treasure chest with new gems.

THE IMPACT OF NEW TECHNOLOGIES

The development of new technologies, computer-based or otherwise, is another area that should continue to facilitate and improve upon the creation and implementation of IBI lessons. In particular, developments in this area should make it increasingly feasible to have learners complete IBI lessons outside of the classroom on their own while still incorporating as many of the principles of the approach as possible. Some of the benefits of this type of independent work are discussed in Chapter 5, particularly with regard to how IBI lessons can be used in conjunction with extensive independent reading outside of class.

What is critical as we move forward with new technologies is to make use of these in a principled and evidence-based manner, keeping in mind how the processing of vocabulary takes place in the learner's mind and not focusing only on how intriguing or nifty the new technology in question may be. The principles of the IBI approach were developed on the shoulders of research and theory related to how learners go about processing and learning vocabulary from a cognitive perspective. Short of the possibility of unique future technologies, such as digital implants that affect language learning and language use in humans, it is unlikely that technological innovations in the (at least) near future will be able to obviate the learning processes responsible for L2 vocabulary learning, processes that the IBI approach was designed to respect and to promote in the most effective manner possible.

AREAS OF RESEARCH ON THE RISE IN ADVANCING UNDERSTANDING OF L2 VOCABULARY LEARNING

In addition to the previously mentioned considerations related to the relationship between the IBI approach, future research, and advances in technology, it may be helpful to consider some particular areas of research related to L2 vocabulary learning that appear to be on the rise and that may have important impacts on the future of understanding L2 vocabulary learning and instruction. This section briefly introduces and discusses three areas of research that should fall within this category: (1) research on the interface between vocabulary (lexis), syntax, and other areas of linguistic competence; (2) research on the quality of L2 vocabulary learning and lexical (or lexicosemantic/form–meaning) representation in the mind; and (3) the neural bases of L2 vocabulary learning and representation. Not only do these areas of research have the potential to impact the approach to vocabulary instruction presented in this book, they have the potential to advance understanding of L2 vocabulary and lexical representation by leaps and bounds. Although it is beyond present purposes to conduct extended reviews of research in these areas, they are introduced briefly here because they are definitely areas to keep an eye on in the future of research related to L2 vocabulary.

The Interface Between Vocabulary and Grammar

In Chapter 1, we considered just a few studies whose findings suggest that much of what we refer to as *grammatical knowledge* actually resides at the level of individual words and combinations thereof: (1) Healy and Sherrod's (1994) finding that English speakers pronounce the word *the* using the schwa phoneme before consonant sounds (*the book, the front*) and the phoneme /i/ before vowel sounds (*the author, the inside*) is based on information stored at the word level; (2) Serwatka and Healy's (1998) finding that English speakers distinguish between count and mass nouns is also based on knowledge at the word level; and (3) Barcroft's (2007b) finding that the ability of native English speakers to make accurate grammaticality judgments decreases dramatically when they change from processing real words (*explained*) to unreal words (*explunned* or *tidnopped*). However, these studies are just a small sampling when it comes to the larger body of work on the relationship, or interface, between vocabulary (lexis) and grammar (syntax).

Consider, for example, the development of *construction grammar*, a theory that opposes any strict distinction between lexis and syntax. Since Lakoff's (1987) classic work on *there*-constructions, in which he argued that the whole of meaning is not the same as the sum of its parts, theoretical advances and research on construction grammar have posited an enormously important role for individual lexical items in the construction of meaning. According to the theory, all form–meaning pairings, including different types of word combinations and idioms (recall the work of Boers [e.g., 2001] from this perspective, as discussed in Chapter 2), are constructions, and grammar (or syntax) consists of a series of constructions. The only difference between words and other constructions is how they are different in terms of the complexity of their internal structure (words often involving less complexity). In this sense lexis and syntax represent extremes of one single continuum. Of course, there are many more aspects to construction grammar to consider, but the denial of this theory of any clear-cut qualitative distinction (except in degree) between words and grammar is another example of the close-knit relationship between what it means to know vocabulary and what it means to know grammar. Readers interested in knowing more about construction grammar are referred to www.constructiongrammar.org.

The Quality of L2 Vocabulary Learning and Representation

Another area in which future research should continue to advance understanding focuses on the quality of L2 vocabulary learning and mental representations for vocabulary in the mind. It is one thing to learn a substantial number of new L2 words. It is another thing whether these words become represented in our minds in a manner that we might like, one that allows for the word forms to be represented naturally or appropriately, such as when word forms are mapped onto their appropriate meanings (their appropriate semantic space) and not mapped onto other meanings or other word forms in a manner that decreases or complicates access, which may lead to less fluent usage.

Consider the Keyword Method of vocabulary learning (Atkinson & Raugh, 1975), a mnemonic technique that involves (in the case of L2 word learning) recoding an L2 word into one or more L1 words and then making a semantic association that helps the learner recall both the form and the meaning. For example, an English-speaking learner of German recodes the novel word form *ecke* into the English word *echo* (the keyword mediator) and creates a mental image of "an echo in the corner" (Ellis & Beaton, 1995, p. 578). Although many (but not all) studies have demonstrated the benefits of using Keyword in terms of quantity of L2 vocabulary learned (e.g., Atkinson & Raugh, 1975; Ellis & Beaton, 1995), others have demonstrated that the Keyword Method has some questionable impacts on the quality of L2 vocabulary learning and how L2 words become represented in the mind.

For example, Kole (2007) examined the qualitative effects of the Keyword Method among English-speaking learners of French using priming and reaction time as a research methodology. The results of the study indicated that keyword mediators continue to be active after learning. For example, learning via keyword caused the French word *maison* ("house") and the English word *maze* to become semantically linked, even though naturalistic learning of the word *maison* would not lead to this type of link (*maison* would come to be linked to the properties of "house," not "maze"). This cost in terms of quality of the representation of L2 words calls into question whether (or at least how often) the Keyword Method should be used. As another example, Barcroft, Sommers, and Sunderman (2011) examined the effects of the Keyword Method (versus rote rehearsal) on the quality of developing L2 word representations in another priming study among English speakers who had never studied Spanish. In this case, it was found that Spanish words learned by rote rehearsal were retrieved faster when they were primed by similar word forms (e.g., *dad* for the Spanish word *dado* ["dice"]) compared to words that were not similar to the target word form, as would be expected. However, words learned via the Keyword Method were retrieved more slowly when primed by similar word forms after those similar word forms were also the keywords used during learning, suggesting that the keywords were activating semantic information related to the keyword.

These demonstrations of the qualitative costs of the Keyword Method speak to the importance of going beyond questions like "How many words were learned?" to include questions such as "How did the words become represented in the mind?" and "How easily are the words now accessed?" Although the IBI approach certainly advocates intentional vocabulary learning and direct teaching of vocabulary, it is not quick to advocate using mnemonic techniques that involve the L1, such as the Keyword Method. As Barcroft et al. (2011) suggest, it is best not to use the Keyword Method for extensive L2 vocabulary learning, but it may be more appropriate on occasion in other contexts, such as when travelers want to remember a key expression or two in a language that they are otherwise not studying or intending to learn with any large degree of proficiency.

In addition to research on the impacts of the Keyword Method on the quality of developing lexical representations, future research on the qualitative impacts of other techniques of vocabulary instruction should be quite informative and have other pedagogical implications. Some areas that come to mind are the qualitative impacts of learning via translation as opposed to learning in L2 only, learning with pictures as opposed to definitions, and learning new vocabulary in the spoken mode as compared to the written mode. It would be helpful to have more data on how instructional differences such as these impact not only the quantity but also the quality of developing lexical representations.

The Neural Bases of L2 Vocabulary Learning and Representation

Finally, a third area in which future research should have a great impact on understanding of L2 vocabulary learning concerns the neural bases that underlie L2 vocabulary learning and representation. What neural processes allow vocabulary learning to occur in the first place? How is vocabulary represented and stored in the brain? What neural processes are involved in accessing vocabulary once it has been stored? These questions have intrigued researchers for a long time, but within the past four decades or so, technological advances—particularly those related to neuroimaging techniques, such as positron emission tomography (PET) and functional magnetic resonance imaging (fMRI), as well as advances in techniques for measuring brain-based electrophysiological responses (electro-encephalography; EEG)—have improved our ability to address such questions. Studies using current technologies in this area cannot answer all of our questions, but they have broken a great deal of new ground during a period of only a few decades. In the not-so-distant future, more fine-grained neuroimaging techniques should continue to facilitate this positive trend.

To provide just one example, consider a neuroimaging study by Jeong et al. (2010) on the location of cortical representation (during retrieval) of L2 vocabulary learned in one of two ways: via written translations (text-based learning) or in the context of real-life situations (situation-based learning). The researchers demonstrated that the cortical areas involved were different in these two contexts (the left-middle frontal gyrus was implicated after text-based learning versus the right supramarginal gyrus after situation-based learning). These findings speak to the importance of the manner in which words are learned when predicting how they will become represented and processed in the brain. Interestingly, in a study on grammar learning, Morgan-Short, Steinhauer, Sanz, and Ullman (2012) demonstrated differential outcomes in type of brain processing due to type of training when comparing the effects of explicit (traditional grammar-focused) versus implicit (not explicit, more communicatively oriented) training on EEG measures (when participants were subsequently asked to make grammaticality judgments related to the structure in question). Only implicit training led to more native-like patterns of EEG responses in this study, pointing again to how critical it is to consider the impact of any type of instruction on the quality of neural representation that the type of instruction in question is likely to promote.

CONCLUDING THOUGHTS

In sum, the future looks bright, at least when it comes to providing the most effective L2 vocabulary instruction possible based on current research and theory. It also looks bright with regard to the potential of new research findings. Innovative research in the future should continue to enhance the capacity to provide effective vocabulary instruction.

The goal of this book has never been *only* to provide instructors with a series of vocabulary activities that they can use in their classrooms. It has been to focus on the *why* of practice—why it is important to present vocabulary repeatedly in the input, why it is important to use meaning-bearing comprehensible input when presenting target words, why it is important to approach vocabulary learning in an incremental but thorough manner. In this sense, this book takes an open-door approach. It is hoped that this approach and the persistent tack toward the *why* of practice both ultimately fit the bill for language instructors.

It is sometimes said that language is the most human thing about being human (e.g., as in the video series "The Human Language," www.equinoxfilms.net /page1.html). It also might be said that vocabulary is the most language-like thing about language. Without minimizing the importance of other linguistic subsystems, vocabulary is truly at the center of language. When teaching individual words and other vocabulary, we focus on what language is at its most foundational level, moving back and forth between lexical form and what it represents (meaning, usage, collocation patterns, etc.). What could be more foundational than this? When an instructor is able to teach effectively at this level, learners tend to respond positively. They intuit and appreciate that they are receiving effective language instruction while working with the very building blocks of language (even when working with less frequently used vocabulary), which increases their ability to communicate effectively in a tangible and immediate sense. The theoretical background, research findings, instructional principles, lesson checklist, and sample lessons presented in this book are intended to support instructors in their efforts to provide this type of instruction on a regular basis.

References

Adelson-Goldstein, J., & Shapiro, N. (2009). *Oxford picture dictionary* (2nd ed.). New York, NY: Oxford.

Arnaud, P. J. L., & Savignon, S. J. (1997). Rare words, complex lexical units, and the advanced learner. In J. Coady & T. Huckin (Eds.), *Second language vocabulary acquisition* (pp. 157–173). Amsterdam, Netherlands: John Benjamins.

Asher, J. J. (1982). *Learning another language through actions.* Los Gatos, CA: Sky Oaks Productions.

Atkinson, R. C., & Raugh, M. R. (1975). An application of the mnemonic keyword method to the acquisition of a Russian vocabulary. *Journal of Experimental Psychology: Human Learning and Memory, 104,* 126–133. doi:10.1037/0278-7393.1.2.126

Bahrick, H. P., Bahrick, L. E., Bahrick, A. S., & Bahrick, P. E. (1993). Maintenance of foreign language vocabulary and the spacing effect. *Psychological Science, 4,* 316–321. doi:10.1111/j.1467-9280.1993.tb00571.x

Barcroft, J. (1998a, April). *The effects of three processing conditions on L2 vocabulary learning.* Paper presented at the Applied Linguistics Colloquium, Department of Spanish, Italian and Portuguese, University of Illinois at Urbana-Champaign, Urbana, IL.

Barcroft, J. (1998b). *L2 vocabulary learning: Do sentence writing and oral repetition help?* Poster presentation at the Second Language Research Forum, Honolulu, HI.

Barcroft, J. (2000). *The effects of sentence writing as semantic elaboration on the allocation of processing resources and second language lexical acquisition* (Unpublished doctoral dissertation). University of Illinois at Urbana-Champaign, Urbana, IL.

Barcroft, J. (2002). Semantic and structural elaboration in L2 lexical acquisition. *Language Learning, 52*(2), 323–363. doi:10.1111/0023-8333.00186

Barcroft, J. (2003a). Distinctiveness and bidirectional effects in input enhancement for vocabulary learning. *Applied Language Learning, 13,* 133–159.

Barcroft, J. (2003b). Effects of questions about word meaning during L2 lexical learning. *Modern Language Journal, 87,* 546–561. doi:10.1111/1540-4781.00207

Barcroft, J. (2004a). Effects of sentence writing in second language lexical acquisition. *Second Language Research, 20,* 303–334. doi:10.1191/0267658304sr233oa

Barcroft, J. (2004b). Promoting second language vocabulary acquisition during reading: Some pivotal issues and eight instructional techniques. *Southern Journal of Linguistics, 26*(2), 94–114.

Barcroft, J. (2004c). Second language vocabulary acquisition: A lexical input processing approach. *Foreign Language Annals, 37,* 200–208. doi:10.1111/j.1944-9720.2004.tb02193.x

Barcroft, J. (2005). La enseñanza del vocabulario en Español como segunda lengua [Vocabulary instruction in Spanish as a second language]. *Hispania, 88,* 568–583. doi:10.2307/20063160

Barcroft, J. (2006). Can writing a new word detract from learning it? More negative effects of forced output during vocabulary learning. *Second Language Research, 22,* 487–497. doi:10.1191/0267658306sr276oa

Barcroft, J. (2007a). Effects of opportunities for word retrieval during second language vocabulary learning. *Language Learning, 57*(1), 35–56. doi:10.1111/j.1467-9922.2007.00398.x

Barcroft, J. (2007b). When knowing grammar depends on knowing words: Native-speaker grammaticality judgments of sentences with real and unreal words. *Canadian Modern Language Review, 63,* 313–343. doi:10.3138/R601-H212-5582-0737

Barcroft, J. (2008). Second language partial word form learning in the written mode. *Estudios de Linguistica Aplicada, 47,* 53–72.

Barcroft, J. (2009). Effects of synonym generation on incidental and intentional vocabulary learning during second language reading. *TESOL Quarterly, 43,* 79–103. doi:10.1002/j.1545-7249.2009.tb00227.x

Barcroft, J., & Rott, S. (2010). Partial word form learning in the written mode in L2 German and Spanish. *Applied Linguistics, 31,* 623–650. doi:10.1093/applin/amq017

Barcroft, J., & Sommers, M. S. (2005). Effects of acoustic variability on second language vocabulary learning. *Studies in Second Language Acquisition, 27,* 387–414. doi:10.1017/S0272263105050175

Barcroft, J., Sommers, M., & Sunderman, G. (2011). Some costs of fooling Mother Nature: A priming study on the keyword method and the quality of developing L2 lexical representations. In P. Trofimovic & K. McDonough (Eds.), *Applying priming research to L2 learning and teaching: Insights from psycholinguistics* (pp. 49–72). Amsterdam, Netherlands: John Benjamins.

Boers, F. (2001). Remembering figurative idioms by hypothesizing about their origin. *Prospect, 16*(3), 35–43.

Boers, F. (2011). Cognitive linguistic approaches to teaching vocabulary: Assessment and integration. *Language Teaching.* doi:10.1017/S0261444811000450

Boers, F., Eyckmans, J., & Stengers, H. (2007). Presenting figurative idioms with a touch of etymology: More than mere mnemonics? *Language Teaching Research, 11,* 43–62. doi:10.1177/1362168806072460

Boers, F., & Lindstromberg, S. (2009). *Optimizing a lexical approach to instructed second language acquisition.* Basingstoke, England: Palgrave Macmillan.

Boers, F., Piquer Píriz, A.-M., Stengers, H., & Eyckmans, J. (2009). Does pictorial elucidation foster recollection of idioms? *Language Teaching Research, 13,* 367–382. doi:10.1177/1362168809341505

Bogaards, P. (2001). Lexical units and the learning of foreign language vocabulary learning. *Studies in Second Language Acquisition, 23,* 321–343. doi:10.1017/S0272263101003011

Brent, M. R., & Siskind, J. M. (2001). The role of exposure to isolated words in early vocabulary development. *Cognition, 81,* B33–B44. doi:10.1016/S0010-0277(01)00122-6

Chen, C., & Truscott, J. (2010). The effects of repetition and L1 lexicalization on incidental vocabulary acquisition. *Applied Linguistics, 31,* 693–713. doi:10.1093/applin/amq031

Coxhead, A. (2000). A new Academic Word List. *TESOL Quarterly, 34,* 213–238. doi:10.2307/3587951

Craik, F. I. M., & Lockhart, R. S. (1972). Levels of processing: A framework for memory research. *Journal of Verbal Learning and Verbal Behavior, 11,* 671–684. doi:10.1016/S0022-5371(72)80001-X

Cruse, D. A. (1986). *Lexical semantics.* New York, NY: Cambridge University Press.

de Groot, A. M. B. (2006). Effects of stimulus characteristics and background music on foreign language vocabulary learning and forgetting. *Language Learning, 56,* 463–506. doi:10.1111/j.1467-9922.2006.00374.x

Ellis, N. (1994). Vocabulary acquisition: The implicit ins and outs of explicit cognitive mediation. In N. Ellis (Ed.), *Implicit and explicit learning of languages* (pp. 211–282). San Diego, CA: Academic Press.

Ellis, N. (2006). Cognitive perspectives on SLA: The associative-cognitive CREED. *AILA Review, 19,* 100–121. doi:10.1075/aila.19.08ell

Ellis, N., & Beaton, A. (1995). Psycholinguistic determinants of foreign language vocabulary learning. In B. Harley (Ed.), *Lexical issues in language learning* (pp. 107–165). Ann Arbor, MI: Benjamins.

Finkbeiner, M., & Nicol, J. (2003). Semantic category effects in second language word learning. *Applied Psycholinguistics, 24,* 369–383. doi:10.1017/S0142716403000195

Folse, K. (2006). The effect of type of written exercise on L2 vocabulary retention. *TESOL Quarterly, 40,* 273–293. doi:10.2307/40264523

Gass, S. (1999). Discussion: Incidental vocabulary learning. *Studies in Second Language Acquisition, 21,* 319–333.

Gorman, T. P. (1979). Teaching reading at the advanced level. In M. Celce-Murcia & L. McIntosh (Eds.), *Teaching English as a foreign language* (pp. 154–162). Rowley, MA: Newbury House.

Haynes, M. (1998, March). *Word form, attention and vocabulary development through reading.* Paper presented at the Annual Conference of the American Association for Applied Linguistics, Seattle, WA.

Hatch, E. (1983). Simplified input and second language acquisition. In R. Andersen (Ed.), *Pidginization and creolization as language acquisition.* Rowley, MA: Newbury House.

Healy, A. F., Barshi, I., Crutcher, R. J., Tao, L., Rickard, T. C., Marmie, W. R., . . . Bourne, L. E., Jr. (1998). Toward the improvement of training in foreign languages. In A. F. Healy & L. E. Bourne Jr. (Eds.), *Foreign language learning: Psycholinguistic studies on training and retention* (pp. 3–53). Mahwah, NJ: Lawrence Erlbaum.

Healy, A. F., & Sherrod, N. B. (1994, November). *The/thee pronunciation distinction: A local model of linguistic categories.* Paper presented at the 35th Annual Meeting of the Psychonomic Society, St. Louis, MO.

Horst, M. (2005). Learning L2 vocabulary through extensive reading: A measurement study. *Canadian Modern Language Review, 61,* 355–382. doi:10.3138/cmlr.61.3.355

Hulstijn, J. H. (1992). Retention of inferred and given word meanings: Experiments in incidental learning. In P. J. L. Arnaud & H. Béjoint (Eds.), *Vocabulary and Applied Linguistics* (pp. 113–125). London, England: Macmillan.

Hulstijn, J. H., Hollander, M., & Greidanus, T. (1996). Incidental vocabulary learning by advanced foreign language students: The influence of marginal glosses, dictionary use, and recurrence of unknown words. *Modern Language Journal, 80,* 327–339. doi:10.2307/329439

Hulstijn, J. H., & Laufer, B. (2001). Some empirical evidence for the involvement load hypothesis in vocabulary acquisition. *Language Learning, 51,* 539–558. doi:10.1111/0023-8333.00164

James, M. (1996). *Improving second language reading comprehension: A computer-assisted vocabulary development approach* (Unpublished doctoral dissertation). University of Hawai'i, Manoa, HI.

Jeong, H., Sugiura, M., Sassa, Y., Wakusawa, K., Horie, K., Sato, S., & Kawashima, R. (2010). Learning second language vocabulary: Neural dissociation of situation-based learning and text-based learning. *NeuroImage, 50,* 802–809. doi:10.1016/j.neuroimage.2009.12.038

Jiang, N. (2000). Lexical representation and development in a second language. *Applied Linguistics, 21,* 47–77. doi:10.1093/applin/21.1.47

Jiang, N. (2004). Semantic transfer and its implications for vocabulary learning in a second language. *Modern Language Journal, 88,* 416–432.

Kelly, L. (1969). *Centuries of language teaching.* Rowley, MA: Newbury House.

Kole, J. A. (2007). *The retrieval process in mediated learning: Using priming effects to test the direct access and covert mediation models* (Unpublished doctoral dissertation). University of Colorado, Boulder, CO.

Krashen, S. (1985). *The input hypothesis: Issues and implications.* New York, NY: Longman.

Krashen, S. (1989). We acquire vocabulary and spelling by reading: Additional evidence for the input hypothesis. *Modern Language Journal, 73,* 440–464. doi:10.2307/326879

Krashen, S. (1993). *The power of reading.* Inglewood, CA: Libraries Unlimited.

Krashen, S., & Terrell, T. (1983). *The natural approach: Language acquisition in the classroom.* Oxford, England: Pergamon.

Lado, R., Baldwin, B., & Lobo, F. (1967). *Massive vocabulary expansion in a foreign language beyond the basic course: The effects of stimuli, timing and order of presentation.* Washington, DC: U.S. Department of Health, Education, and Welfare.

Lakoff, G. (1987). *Women, fire, and dangerous things: What categories reveal about the mind.* Chicago, IL: University of Chicago Press.

Lakoff, G., & Johnson, M. (1980). *Metaphors we live by.* Chicago, IL: University of Chicago Press.

Laufer, B., & Hulstijn, J. (2001). Incidental vocabulary acquisition in a second language: The construct of task-induced involvement. *Applied Language Learning, 22,* 1–26. doi:10.1093/applin/22.1.1

Lee, J. F., & VanPatten, B. (1995). *Making communicative language teaching happen* (1st edition). New York, NY: McGraw-Hill.

Lee, J. F., & VanPatten, B. (2003). *Making communicative language teaching happen* (2nd edition). New York, NY: McGraw-Hill.

Lewis, M. (1993). *The lexical approach: The state of ELT and the way forward.* Hove, England: Language Teaching Publications.

Lewis, M. (1997). Pedagogical implications of the lexical approach. In J. Coady & T. Huckin (Eds.), *Second language vocabulary acquisition* (pp. 255–270). Cambridge, England: Cambridge University Press.

Liu, N., & Nation, I. S. P. (1985). Factors affecting guessing in context. *RELC Journal, 16,* 33–42. doi:10.1177/003368828501600103

Long, M. (Ed.). (2005). *Second language needs analysis.* Cambridge, England: Cambridge University Press.

Luppescu, S., & Day, R. (1993). Reading, dictionaries, and vocabulary learning. *Language Learning, 43,* 263–287. doi:10.1111/j.1467-1770.1992.tb00717.x

Martinez, R., & Schmitt, N. (2011, July). The phrase list (and what it can do). Paper presented at the 9th Southern Cone TESOL Convention. Retrieved from http://sfsu.academia.edu/RonMartinez/Talks/46798/The_Phrasal_Expressions_List_PHRASE_List_and_what_it_can_do_for_you

Martinez, R., & Schmitt, N. (2012). A phrasal expressions list. *Applied Linguistics, 33*(3), 299–320. doi:10.1093/applin/ams010

McNamara, D. S., & Healy, A. F. (1995). A generation advantage for multiplication skill training and nonword vocabulary acquisition. In A. F. Healy & L. E. Bourne Jr. (Eds.), *Learning and memory of knowledge and skills: Durability and specificity* (pp. 132–169). Thousand Oaks, CA: Sage.

Meara, P. (1980). Vocabulary acquisition: A neglected aspect of language learning. *Language Teaching and Linguistics: Abstracts 13,* 221–246. doi:10.1017/S0261444800008879

Mondria, J.-A., & Mondria-De Vries, S. (1994). Efficiently memorizing words with the help of word cards and "hand computer": Theory and applications. *System, 22,* 47–57. doi:10.1016/0346-251X(94)90039-6

Morgan-Short, K., Steinhauer, K., Sanz, C., & Ullman, M. T. (2012). Explicit and implicit second language training differentially affect the achievement of native-like brain activation patterns. *Journal of Cognitive Neuroscience, 24,* 933–947. doi:10.1162/jocn_a_00119

Morris, C. D., Bransford, J. D., & Franks, J. J. (1977). Levels of processing versus transfer appropriate processing. *Journal of Verbal Learning and Verbal Behavior, 16,* 519–533. doi:10.1016/S0022-5371(77)80016-9

Murphy, R. (with Smalzer, W. R.). (2009). *Grammar in use: Intermediate* (3rd ed.). Singapore: Cambridge.

Nagy, W. (1997). On the role of context in first- and second-language vocabulary learning. In N. Schmitt & M. McCarthy (Eds.), *Vocabulary: Description, acquisition, and pedagogy* (pp. 64–83). Cambridge, England: Cambridge University Press.

Nagy, W., Anderson, R., & Herman, P. (1987). Learning words from context during normal reading. *American Educational Research Journal, 24,* 237–270. doi:10.3102/00028312024002237

Nakata, T. (2011). Computer-assisted second language vocabulary learning in a paired-associate paradigm: A critical investigation of flashcard software. *Computer Assisted Language Learning, 24,* 17–38. doi:10.1080/09588221.2010.520675

Nation, I. S. P. (2001). *Learning vocabulary in another language.* Cambridge, England: Cambridge University Press.

Nation, I. S. P., & Waring, R. (1997). Vocabulary size, text coverage and word lists. In N. Schmitt & M. McCarthy (Eds.), *Vocabulary: Description, acquisition and pedagogy* (pp. 238–254). Amsterdam, Netherlands: John Benjamins.

Oxford University Press. (2006). *Oxford English corpus.* Retrieved from http://oxforddictionaries.com/words/the-oxford-english-corpus

Paribakht, T. S., & Wesche, M. (1997). Vocabulary enhancement activities and reading for meaning in second language vocabulary acquisition. In J. Coady & T. Huckin (Eds.), *Second language vocabulary acquisition* (pp. 174–200). Amsterdam, Netherlands: John Benjamins.

Paribakht, T. S., & Wesche, M. (1999). Reading and "incidental" L2 vocabulary acquisition: An introspective study of lexical inferencing. *Studies in Second Language Acquisition, 21,* 195–224.

Pigada, M., & Schmitt, N. (2006). Vocabulary acquisition from extensive reading: A case study. *Reading in a Foreign Language, 18,* 1–28.

Politzer, E. (1978). Errors of English speakers of German as perceived and evaluated by German natives. *Modern Language Journal, 62,* 253–261. doi:10.1111/j.1540-4781.1978.tb02395.x

Prince, P. (1996). Second language vocabulary learning: The role of context versus translations as a function of proficiency. *Modern Language Journal, 80,* 478–493. doi:10.1111/j.1540-4781.1996.tb05468.x

Pulido, D. (2003). Modeling of the role of second language proficiency and topic familiarity in L2 incidental vocabulary acquisition through reading. *Language Learning, 53,* 233–284.

Richards, J. (1976). The role of vocabulary teaching. *TESOL Quarterly, 10,* 77–89. doi:10.2307/3585941

Richards, J., & Rodgers, T. S. (1986). *Approaches and methods in language teaching: A description and analysis.* New York, NY: Cambridge University Press.

Rott, S. (1999). The effect of exposure frequency on intermediate language learners' incidental vocabulary acquisition and retention through reading. *Studies in Second Language Acquisition, 21,* 589–619. doi:10.1017/S0272263199004039

Royer, J. M. (1973). Memory effects for test-like events during acquisition of foreign language vocabulary. *Psychological Reports, 32,* 195–198. doi:10.2466/pr0.1973.32.1.195

Schmitt, N. (2010). *Researching vocabulary: A vocabulary research manual.* Hampshire, England: Palgrave Macmillan.

Schmitt, N., Schmitt, D., & Clapham, C. (2001). Developing and exploring the behavior of two new versions of the Vocabulary Levels Test. *Language Testing, 18(1)*, 55–88. doi:10.1177/026553220101800103

Serwatka, M., & Healey, A. F. (1998). On the status of the count-mass distinction in a mental grammar. In A. F. Healy & L. E. Bourne Jr. (Eds.), *Foreign language learning: Psycholinguistic studies on training and retention* (pp. 113–140). Mahwah, NJ: Lawrence Erlbaum.

Sharwood Smith, M. (1991). Speaking to many minds: On the relevance of different types of language information for the L2 learner. *Second Language Research, 7*, 118–132. doi:10.1177/026765839100700204

Sinclair, J. M., & Renouf, A. (1988). A lexical syllabus for language learning. In R. Carter & M. McCarthy (Eds.), *Vocabulary and language teaching* (pp. 140–158). Harlow, England: Longman.

Slamecka, N. J., & Graf, P. (1978). The generation effect: Delineation of a phenomenon. *Journal of Experimental Psychology, 4*, 592–604. doi:10.1037/0278-7393.4.6.592

Smith, R. C. (2007). Michael West's life and career. Retrieved from http://www2 .warwick.ac.uk/fac/soc/al/research/collect/elt_archive/halloffame/west/life/

Soars, L., & Soars, J. (2005). *New headway: Upper-intermediate student's book* (3rd ed.). Oxford, England: Oxford.

Sommers, M. S., & Barcroft, J. (2007). An integrated account of the effects of acoustic variability in first language and second language: Evidence from amplitude, fundamental frequency, and speaking rate variability. *Applied Psycholinguistics, 28*, 231–249. doi:10.1017/S0142716407070129

Thomas, M. H., & Dieter, J. N. (1987). The positive effects of writing practice on integration of foreign words in memory. *Journal of Educational Psychology, 79*, 249–253. doi:10.1037/0022-0663.79.3.249

Tinkham, T. (1997). The effects of semantic and thematic clustering on the learning of second language vocabulary learning. *Second Language Research, 13*, 138–163. doi:10.1191/026765897672376469

Webb, S. (2008). The effects of context on incidental vocabulary learning. *Reading in a Foreign Language, 20*, 232–245.

West, M. (1953). *A general service list of English words*. London, England: Longman.

Wilkins, D. (1972). *Linguistics in language teaching*. London, England: Arnold.

Willis, D. (1990). *The lexical syllabus: A new approach to language teaching*. London, England: Collins ELT.

Wong, W. (2005). *Input enhancement: From theory and research to the classroom*. New York, NY: McGraw-Hill.

Wong, W., & Pyun, D. O. (2012). The effects of sentence writing on L2 French and Korean lexical acquisition. *Canadian Modern Language Review, 68,* 164–189. doi:10.3138/cmlr.68.2.164

Yamamoto, Y. (2011). Bridging the gap between receptive and productive vocabulary size through extensive reading. *The Reading Matrix, 11,* 226–242.

Yun, J. (2010). *The effects of hypertext glosses on L2 vocabulary acquisition: A meta-analysis* (Doctoral dissertation). Available from ProQuest Dissertations and theses database. (UMI No. 3409527)

Zimmerman, C. (1997). Historical trends in second language vocabulary instruction. In J. Coady & T. Huckin (Eds.), *Second language vocabulary acquisition* (pp. 5–19). Amsterdam, Netherlands: John Benjamins.

Index

Also Available From TESOL

More Than a Native Speaker
and
From Language Learner to Language Teacher
Don Snow

❋ ❋ ❋ ❋ ❋

TESOL Classroom Practice Series
Maria Dantas-Whitney, Sarah Rilling, and Lilia Savova, Series Editors

❋ ❋ ❋ ❋ ❋

Language Teacher Development Series
Thomas S. C. Farrell, Series Editor

❋ ❋ ❋ ❋ ❋

New Ways in TESOL Series
Jack C. Richards, Series Editor

❋ ❋ ❋ ❋ ❋

TESOL Language Curriculum Development Series
Kathleen Graves, Series Editor

❋ ❋ ❋ ❋ ❋

TESOL Standards

- *Preparing Effective Teachers of English Language Learners: Practical Applications for the TESOL P–12 Professional Teaching Standards*

- *Standards for Adult Education ESL Programs*

- *Standards for ESL/EFL Teachers of Adults*

- *TESOL Technology Standards: Description, Implementation, Integration*

- *PreK–12 English Language Proficiency Standards*
  Augmentation of the World-Class Instructional Design and Assessment (WIDA) Consortium
  English Language Proficiency Standards

To Order or Request a Review Copy

Online: www.tesol.org "Read and Publish"
Email: tesolpubs@brightkey.net
Toll Free Phone: +1 888-891-0041 (United States)
Mail: TESOL Publications, 9050 Junction Drive
Annapolis Junction, MD 20701 USA